love of enemy

The Cross And Sword Trial

LEONARD DESROCHES

Love of Enemy
Copyright © 2019 by Leonard Desroches

All rights reserved. No part of this publication may be reproduced, distributed, or transmitted in any form or by any means, including photocopying, recording, or other electronic or mechanical methods, without the prior written permission of the author, except in the case of brief quotations embodied in critical reviews and certain other non-commercial uses permitted by copyright law.

Tellwell Talent
www.tellwell.ca

ISBN
978-0-2288-1708-6 (Paperback)

Contents

Foreword
Thanks
Introduction

1 Water breaking through
Before the public witness: a context

2 Cross and ploughshare or cross and sword?
A brief history of the public witness

3 A Cloud of witnesses
The trial
THE WITNESSES
THE ACCUSED
THE JUDGEMENT

4 Prison walls, church walls and freedom
Personal reflections on the aftermath

National Library of Canada Cataloguing in Publication

Desroches, Leonard, 1948-

Love of enemy: the cross and sword trial/
Leonard Desroches

ISBN:

1. Cross and Sword Trial, Toronto, Ont., 2000.
2. Desroches, Leonard, 1948-
–Trials, litigation, etc.
3. Heap, Don, 1925-2014 – Trials, litigation, etc.
4. Holmes, Bob, 1936 – Trials litigation, etc.
5. Christian Peacemaker Teams
6. St. Paul's Anglican Church (Toronto, Ont.)
7. Just war doctrine
8. Nonviolence–Religious aspects
–Christianity
I. Title

KE229.C47D48 2002
345.71'0264
C2002-901857-9

to Anna

*and to the memory
and new presence of*

Adolphe Proulx

*beloved bishop of
Gatineau-Hull, Québec
b. December 12, 1927
d. July 22, 1987*

Foreword

Daniel Berrigan

I went through the manuscript with a deepening sense that I was opening a gift of import. As indeed I was!

The story of 'The Cross and Sword Trial' brought home with force the price of living a principled life, whether in the American empire or its imperial satellite, Canada. The latter alas, tending so dependably to ape the thuggish ways of its southern mentor.

The complicity of the churches in such murky matters is in no need of elaboration. We of the U.S. are presently at the untender mercies of a most bellicose secular arm. It rains indiscriminate hammer blows from the skies, on innocent and guilty alike in tormented Afghanistan.

And as if that were not a sufficient penance, the Catholic bishops, hundreds of them, have stood foursquare behind the gratuitous, grotesque assault, the search and destroy mission after a demonised enemy.

The history is there, as 'The Cross and Sword Trial' demonstrates. On the forge of Mars, the past is melded to the awful present, church and state, north and south.

If this were all, if the church were as paganised and blinded as appears, we were indeed without hope. But the American bishops do not exhaust or eviscerate the Christian story, as lived and practised. In Canada and the U.S., other Christians challenge, clairvoyantly and courageously, the 'might makes right' savageries of officialdom.

Among such Christians, Leonard and his fellow defendants honourably stand. They give us solid grounds for hope, amid the institutionalised despair of doctored polls and mesmerised media.

The Gospel lives. The news is new—and God knows, it is good.

Thanks

Serious exploration of love of enemy is a near-taboo for the right, left and centre—both religious and secular. That doesn't leave a lot of people.

I am grateful for those who were willing to support the birthing of this book—financially and otherwise. Your support is especially precious since no publisher wanted to risk publishing it. One major Christian publishing house showed great interest for months. But after the September 11 massacre in the U.S.A. they decided to back off. Some other publishers actually praised the manuscript while refusing to publish it themselves, saying, "Have you tried other publishers?" I recall the words of Chan Tin, a Catholic Vietnamese priest, referring to the relentless persistence required after his presses had been destroyed during the American war in Vietnam: "Our ancestors printed on palm leaves when necessary."

The task of self-publishing is extremely time-consuming and expensive. It would have been quite simply impossible without the financial assistance of the following: the Dominican Friars of Toronto; Don Warne; Ed and Rena Newbery; Kevin Doyle; the Edmonton Grey Nuns; Mary Kehoe; Carmen Gravelle, psm, and her community; the Basilians; Annette Oudejans; the Providence Sisters east and west; the Presentation Sisters; the Sisters of St. Joseph of Pembroke and the participants at their March 2002 retreat; Sister Mary Ellen Francoeur; Menai Wardle; Sister Amanda Desharnais and the CRC Manitoba; Jocelyn Fallu, FDLS and her community; Murray Thomson; Paul Flanagan; Rev. Canon Bruce Mutch; Don and Hester Warne; Gerald Lepp; Dr. Bruce Robertson; Charles Bryant; Elizabeth Urtnowski; Professor Ron Dart; David Ramsey; Maureen Morette; the Grey Sisters of Ottawa and participants at their Kairos Centre February 2002 workshop; Maria Heynan; Jo Anne, Teresa, Mary and Jeane of the Sisters of St. Joseph, Toronto.

Thanks to those who helped with the editing work: Vivian Harrower, Naomi Gold and Jim Loney.

I always enjoy collaborating with Willem Hart, talented and generous graphic designer. Speaking of artist friends, thanks to Jo Roberts of the Toronto Catholic Worker and to Wayne Karlstedt for their excellent photos; and to Christopher Reilly for his inspired drawings.

Thanks to Bernard Ménard, omi and Jim Creskey for assistance in finding a printer; to Sheila at Another Story bookstore for her general book world advice.

Thanks to my co-worker, Jim Carey-Hill for his valued support while I took time from my drywall work to attend to the long birthing.

Thanks to the Trappist monks at Rogersville, N.B., for their brotherly hospitality.

A special note of gratitude to the witnesses at our trial: Bishop Thomas Gumbleton, Ms. Janet Somerville and Reverend Jeannie Loughrey.

Throughout the many months of the Cross and Sword Witness Bob Holmes, Don Heap and I were richly blessed by a faithful community of supporters—only a few of whom are mentioned in the body of this book.

We remain grateful for every single one of you.

Introduction

This book is a meditation on the urgent, life-giving mystery at the heart of justice—making and nonviolent resistance to evil and terrorism: the love of enemy to which Christ calls us. Necessarily, it confronts us with the church teaching of "Just War."

This examination is presented through a nonviolent witness which lasted from 1998 to 2000 and which culminated in the *Cross and Sword Trial* in Toronto, Canada involving Bishop Thomas Gumbleton of Detroit, Michigan, other church people, and many supporters.

The first chapter situates the issue of Just War in a broader historical and cultural context. Chapter two recounts the story of our nonviolent witness: *who* (the three of us directly involved; the supporters; those affected by the action; and finally the trial witnesses); *what* (urging the mainline churches to take down a sword superimposed on a cross and turn it into a ploughshare as a public commitment to the renunciation of all war); plus the story's *when*, *where*, *how*, and *why*. The next chapter—the heart of the book—presents the trial: the accused, the witnesses and the judgement—along with a stunning cloud of testimonies revealing some of the depth and breadth of love and enemy. The final chapter includes a very brief update; some reflections and conclusions; plus a major proposal to the mainline Christian denominations.

The church community, in the face of global injustice and terrorism, has become spiritually impoverished and weak after centuries of "justified", "just", and "holy" wars. Christ offers radical freedom—far from the degrading lies, debilitating myths and false solutions of the institution of war. This work attempts to explore that freedom. Whether one reads all the chapters, or only the one dealing with the trial, my hope is that this book will contribute to an understanding of gospel nonviolence through a communal meditation on the most feared, and yet urgent, of mysteries: love of enemy.

Leonard Desroches
Toronto, May 2002

1 Water breaking through

Before the public witness: a context

"A spring deep inside…"

Nobel Laureate Mairead Corrigan Maguire looked up at the ceiling of the community centre in West Baghdad where nearly 1200 women, children and elderly men had been incinerated in seconds by a U.S. "smart bomb." Where the top bunks of a children's dormitory had been she could see the charred prints of hands and fingernails where children had desperately tried to claw their way out before they burned to death. She had seen that before—in the "shower houses" of Auschwitz.

This is one of a number of searing eyewitness experiences which Jesuit priest John Dear described as then-director of the Fellowship of Reconciliation-U.S.A. (FOR-U.S.A.) and participant in fact-finding missions in Iraq.

As a Canadian, the Gulf War of 1991 was for me a sickening display of our usually less visible day-to-day warmaking: selling of arms to brutal dictatorships; hypocritical reliance on the U.S. nuclear weapons system; profiteering from the design, production, promotion and sale of parts for the U.S. military-industrial-educational complex.

There was something especially painful, but undoubtedly necessary, about being so bluntly reminded of the ultimate purpose of our military as our own fighter jets participated directly in the bombing of Iraqi children, women and men—with Cruise missiles whose navigational systems had been built at Litton Systems, just outside of Toronto. There was something especially offensive about our government's cowardice and utter incapacity to follow a course independent of the U.S. empire. (The small country of New Zealand has been far more courageous in paying the price for charting its own independent military course. In 1984 it was excluded from an alliance with the United States and Australia for refusing to allow nuclear-capable allied warships to visit its ports. Despite strong pressure, it has not abandoned this policy. Recently, New Zealand again risked the wrath of its allies with plans to strip its air force of fighter jets and sharply reduce its navy.)

At the onset of the Gulf War, I joined a number of groups in acts of resistance. I participated in *Pax Chisti Canada's* powerful and imaginative demonstration and nonviolent civil disobedience action in front of the U.S. Embassy. Blocking traffic with a silent march, we beat empty oil drums to point to the killing for oil. I also joined friends from the Toronto Catholic Worker and Scarboro Foreign Missions in an Ash Wednesday resistance action: the pouring of ashes at the entrance of the Conservative Party's Toronto headquarters. There were arrests and court appearances.

Through it all I felt an intense call to engage in a public fast. For three weeks before Easter, I fasted in a public prayer space where anyone was welcome to come and pray. Some came for a few minutes; some for many hours. Some cried; some raged. Some simply tried to stop running away from the mad truth: we are a warmaking country, ready to commit mass murder for the U.S.A's oil!

In May of 1997, after the deaths of hundreds of thousands of Iraqis through economic sanctions, I invited a group of Christians from various denominational backgrounds to come together and explore nonviolent direct action in the context of faith. We referred to ourselves as a "Faith and Resistance Group." Each one in the group was already involved with some kind of justice work. Resistance as such was new to most. We came together to confront the globalization of greed. We tried to understand our own complicity as members of the Christian community, and also to take seriously our particular spiritual resources and rich traditions of resistance to injustice. Realizing that the violence of the rule of wealth is massive, we saw that the need for resistance is urgent.

A number of months into this exploration, the Canadian government threatened to participate in a second bombing of Iraqi civilians in January 1998. For a week, this sickening display of abusive power, funded by Canadian workers' money, affected everything I tried to do. I went into deep spiritual mourning.

On my way to a meeting to discuss our next steps as a group, something happened that made it painfully impossible for me to go on with our regular planning process.

I was confronted by a symbol that almost perfectly symbolizes what we have allowed ourselves to become as a faith community: a cross with a sword at the very centre-part of a war memorial on the front yard of a local church. As a church we preach the radical love symbolized by the Cross, but we cling to the right of the Sword's massive killing, called war. I had previously been very affected by this Cross and Sword Symbol (officially named the "Cross of Sacrifice") during the three-week Lenten fast at the beginning of the Gulf War. But this time something was ripped open inside me. Not blood, but water came flooding out of me.

Though I was aware of my strong feeling related to this symbol, I truly was surprised by the sheer torrent in my soul. I stopped everything that I was doing and spent many hours in prayer and discernment. I had resisted warmaking at the doorsteps of corporations and governments for many years. But now I realized, with an intensity never before felt, that unless I confronted my own church community's complicity, I could never hope to radically address the perpetuation of war and its false economy.

War disrupts everything—a longed-for visit to grandma, a much-needed holiday, the sacred planting of crops, careers, weddings—and, yes, even the best of meetings.

I put before the group my conviction that I could not *not* resist this warmaking which was sanctioned and perpetuated by the churches' Just War teaching. I discussed this war memorial and asked if anyone else felt called to engage in an act of resistance directed specifically at the church itself. Two priests, one Anglican and one Roman Catholic, did feel called to join in such a witness.

Through a difficult discipline, our group confronted how this relentless massacre in Iraq was disrupting our own planned process. As a group we continued organizing a major *three-week public Lenten fast*, which we had just decided on, aimed at exposing and *denouncing the*

Scott McLoughlin-Marratto and Mary Gauthier, OLM take our prayerful cry against greed to the heart of wealth-making at Bay and King Streets, downtown Toronto.

globalization of greed. The fast took place in a church located in the heart of Toronto's bank towers. Everyone participated as best they could. Through much imagination and hard work the fast proved to be for all of us a deepening of our lives and an honest public witness against the real violence of greed.

After the fast, the three of us—Bob Holmes, Don (Dan) Heap and myself—began to prepare for what was to become known as the "Cross and Sword" witness and action. Throughout the action, much-valued supporters helped with the vital tasks. Though I rarely take part in groups composed of only men, this time it seemed fitting that three men, deeply involved in the church's life, should take responsibility for the centuries of male-dominated theological justifications for Just War teachings.

The next chapter will tell the story of who we are, what we set out to do and how we went about it—the retreats, meetings, vigils, fasts and two arrests.

First, it seems important to give a wider context of the relationship between War and Church. For the sake of simplicity, the war in Iraq will be the main reference point, simply because it is almost impossible to keep up with the relentless warmaking in the world. (As I write this, I am discerning how to stretch to respond to a request to lead a nonviolence training session for young people from Congo, where three million people have perished in a nightmarish slaughter involving six different armies and eleven ethnic groups. Today three million in Congo—with barely an outcry; yesterday three million Jews in Poland—with barely an outcry.)

The war in Iraq will serve as the particular example, but it is the very Institution of War that is being considered throughout.

"We drink from our own wells"
The early church's radical spiritual wisdom

War Versus Faith
Caius Julius Caesar, Roman general and dictator (100-44 BCE), who slaughtered 430,000 Germans in one battle, once declared, "Men are nearly always willing to believe what they wish." It must have amazed and greatly pleased him how quickly the mass mind can be constructed. With the help of a little propaganda of fear and greed, how quickly people will hand over their power to someone else in false obedience and follow orders. How quickly thousands of men (and now women!) can be sent to kill and be killed, en masse: young peasants setting aside familiar plough for cold sword to kill unknown young peasants; young computer experts killing unknown young computer experts with high-tech "smart" bombs, not mere primitive swords.

Origen, a theologian of the early church community, stated: "The greatest warfare is not with human enemies, but with those forces which make people into enemies." In the third century after Christ, the young war resister Maximilian declared to the Roman proconsul Dion, in North Africa: "I will not be a soldier…I am a Christian." Given the death penalty, he shouted, "God lives!"

The early church community understood the necessity of facing principalities and powers, rather than simplifying evil by demonizing individuals or groups. They understood that speaking truth to principalities and powers meant that "*When* [not *if*] they take you before synagogues and magistrates and authorities, do not worry about how to defend yourselves or what to say, because when the time comes, the Holy Spirit will teach you what you must say."

In spite of U.S. attempts to demonize Sadaam Hussein, the Iraqi leader's record for torture, arbitrary detention and unwarranted executions is, unfortunately, the norm for that region, according to *Amnesty International's* 1997 report on the Middle East. Further, the Washington-based *Henry L. Stimson Center* reckons that at least 11 other countries besides Iraq have biological warfare capacity. It is not as simple an issue as a monster called Hussein. It goes much deeper into our collective soul. It is about "principalities and powers." Only the soul force of active nonviolence can fully confront evil. As Martin Luther King put it, "Hatred cannot drive out hatred. Only love can do that." By allowing one Iraqi child to die every minute as a direct result of economic sanctions, in order to get back at a "monster", the West has become mired in a futile attempt to drive out hatred with hatred.

The witness of the early church community against the institution of war is dramatic. The voices are many: "We who used to kill one another, do not make war on our enemies. We have each changed our instruments of war, our swords into ploughshares, and our spears into farming tools." – Justin Marty (c.138); "Christ, in disarming Peter, ungirt every soldier. How will a Christian take part in war, nay, how will he serve even in peace?" – Tertullian (c.160–c.225); "Murder, which in the case of an individual is admitted to be a crime, is called a virtue when it is committed wholesale." – Cyprian (d.258).

The brutal military economy of empire versus the loaves and fishes
In his *Orationes Philippicae, V,* Cicero noted that "The sinews of war are infinite money"—what we call taxes. For the first three centuries the early church community understood this and refused to cooperate with the military economy of the empire. They understood power as radical service—power with, not power over. Clement of Alexandria (c.150–c.215) was clear about which kind of economy the early church community was involved in: "We are trained not for war, but for peace." Trained in the radical sharing of the loaves and fishes. Trained in the intricate science and art of cooperation.

Far from seeing power as automatically negative, this was a faith community fully alive with a vision of genuine power as compassion, justice, mercy and radical service; power as soul force. The early Greek church community differentiated between two expressions of power: *dunamis*, the inner, God-given power that we are all created with—dignity; and *exousia*, socially-sanctioned power—public authority (which may or may not be good, depending on the extent to which it is expressed as radical service). This was a community helping to give birth to a radically new understanding of power.

The great Abortion: from faith community to state religion
In 313 CE, Emperor Constantine issued the Edict of Milan making Christianity and other faiths openly legal. Jerome (c.342–420) noted: "As the church increased in influence, it decreased in Christian virtues." Episcopalian theologian Carter Heyward reflected that the church "lost a major element of its identity: its role as a body of resistance to oppressive power relations."

In fact, by 420, when Christianity was becoming the "official" religion, it had begun to persecute heresies. A mere 16 years later, in 436, only Christians could serve in the Roman army. The transformation was now complete: from faith community to official state religion; from persecuted church to religious army. The Roman army was now 100% Christian. The Cross and the Sword were united—and have remained officially united to this day.

From "Justified Wars," to "Just Wars," to "Holy Wars,"
to "M.A.D.—Mutually Assured Destruction"
In the period of the Edict of Milan, a powerful civil administrator from that city, a man named Ambrose, became a Christian. He later became the bishop of Milan. His writings drew greatly on Cicero's *De officiis* ("*On Social Roles*"). Ambrose's writings in turn greatly influenced that of the renowned teacher Augustine (354–430), who wrote at great length about what has come to be known as the Just War concept.

Augustine also developed the principle of "*compelle intrare*"—forced conversion. In the 12th century, the tremendously influential Cistercian monk, St. Bernard de Clairvaux, son of a pious knight, at first hesitated, but then accepted this notion of "*compelle intrare*." In 1145, one of Bernard's former monks became Pope Eugene III. The pope called on Bernard to preach the Second Crusade. After some reluctance, Bernard did so with enthusiasm. Bernard was revered for his powerful sermons to the Christian warriors, the crusaders. He wrote the *Ad Milites Templi*, which was considered by some to be the 'breviary' of warfare for Christian knights. It is literally a manual of how proper Christian killing of enemies should take place. Preaching to the Second Crusade, St. Bernard declared: "No doubt the death of a saint is always precious in the eyes of God, wherever it occurs. But doesn't it seem even more especially beautiful on a battle field, where its glory is greater?"

In direct contrast to Bernard, Francis of Assisi, having fought in two bloody wars, had no illusions about the sanctity of war. Having languished in jail as a political prisoner, he also had no illusions about the glory of war. After his conversion—his encounter with Christ—Francis renounced all war. This is especially remarkable because the crusades reached their climax during Francis' lifetime. The crusade preached by St. Bernard had been a disaster. So was the third one. In August 1198, Innocent III issued a call for the Fourth Crusade (1202–1204). It also failed miserably. In April of 1213, Innocent III wrote his most important encyclical, *Quia maior*, calling on the whole of Christendom to prepare for the Fifth Crusade, which was to take place in 1217–1221. This was encyclical was an intensive, all-out effort to mobilize the material and spiritual forces of all Christians. It is striking how not a trace of these war teachings can be found in the writings of Francis, even though other papal writings on preaching, penance and the Eucharist clearly influenced what he wrote.

The renunciation of all war and its false economy was part of the very foundation of Francis' conversion to a life of radical simplicity in community with brothers who earned their living with good work, and who shared their lives with the marginalized. Francis, and the thousands who joined his community, are acknowledged by some historians as having contributed to the dismantling of an oppressive feudal economy. From an extremely privileged upper middle-class merchant and part-time warrior, Francis became "*Il Fraticello*,"—the "Little Brother," to all. The stranger and the enemy—the "other"—became "Sister" and "Brother." The wondrous, sensuous, physical world of creation, often feared and therefore despised in the time of Francis, became "Sister Water," "Brother Fire." Death revealed the fuller meaning of freedom and became "Sister Bodily Death—whom no one can escape."

In July of 1219, after his conversion, Francis was in Acre on his way to Damietta, Egypt, where the crusaders had begun a siege a year earlier. Before Francis' arrival in March, the Egyptian Sultan, a Saracen Muslim named Melek-al-Kamil, had offered peace talks with generous conditions: transfer of Jerusalem to the Christians in exchange for their evacuation from Egypt. The commander of the Christian warriors, papal delegate Cardinal Pelagius Galvani, bishop of Albano, rejected the offer. In May 1218 the crusaders began their siege of Damietta.

Francis went vulnerable and unarmed to meet the enemy, Melek-al-Kamil. Both men were profoundly affected by this encounter. Francis then turned to the Christian crusaders. Thomas of Celano recounts in his *Second Life* how Francis "approached the Christians…forbidding the war and denouncing the reason for it. But truth was turned to ridicule, and they hardened their hearts…" On November 5, 1219, Damietta fell to the Christians. Of the 80,000 men, women and children living in the city, about 3,000 were left alive after the massacre by the Christian warriors. All but 100 of the survivors were wounded.

The unattended, festering division within the churches
In the face of war the mainline church community of today is still as profoundly divided as at the time of Bernard of Clairvaux and Francis of Assisi. Francis' challenge is still being turned to ridicule. Books are still being written about Bernard that fail to address his war sermons and his manual on how to kill enemies. How telling it is that we know so little about another Cistercian abbot, Isaac of L'Etoile: he was a pacifist who condemned the crusades and who denounced the formation of the military "Orders" of monks, calling them a *monstrum novum*, a "new monstrosity." This Cistercian was completely out of step with the papacy.

It is an illusion to see ourselves as a united church community when it comes to the question of war. We have yet to face our profound division.

The false teaching of *compelle intrare* has sanctioned the very foundation of militarism here in the Americas: the millions of First Nations people whom the Christians enslaved, tortured and murdered. It is on this bloody foundation that much of our wealth has been built. Dominican Bishop Bartolomé de las Casas, a Spaniard and a contemporary of Christopher Columbus, dedicated his entire life defending the dignity of indigenous people. He wrote of the effects of *compelle intrare* in his treatise, *A Very Brief Account of the Destruction of the Indies*:

> In the year 1511, the Spaniards passed over to the island of Cuba, saying, "Princes and Indians…we make known unto you that there is one God, one Pope, and one King

> of Castile, who is lord of this country. Come and render him obedience…otherwise know that we shall make war on you…" They attacked the town, setting fire to the houses that were usually of straw, burning the children, the women, and many others alive…Then when the fire was extinguished or low they went to look for the gold that was in the houses.

He goes on to list horror after horror, like someone witnessing Nazi atrocities.

Today, after centuries of *compelle intrare*, we have NATO, an organization of countries of mainly Western Christian heritage. On February 11, 1999, I heard a CBC report announcing that NATO would bomb the Serbs if they did not sign a peace accord. Be peaceful or we will bomb you! Fighting hatred with hatred.

On April 9, 1999, 19 Serbia-based groups issued a letter strongly condemning the NATO bombing: "We, the representatives of civil groups and organizations, have courageously and consistently fought against every warmongering and nationalistic policy, and for the respect of human rights, and particularly against the repression of Kosovo Albanians…The NATO intervention has destroyed everything that has been achieved so far and the very survival of the civil society in Serbia." Vojin Dimitrijevic, former Vice Chairman of the UN Human Rights Committee and member of the Belgrade Centre for Human Rights declared that the NATO bombing had "erased in one night the results of 10 years of hard work of groups of courageous people in the non-governmental organizations and in the democratic opposition, who have tried to develop institutions of civil society, to promote liberal and civic values and to teach non-violent conflict resolution."

NATO marked its 50th anniversary in 1999. Canadian Undersecretary Escott Reid inspired the birth of NATO. He and other Canadians helped to conceptualize it, push for it and shape it into being on April 4, 1949.

Poisoned waters—the institution of war and the globalization of greed

Questioning the war propaganda
In 1998, at least two of Canada's most experienced soldiers disagreed strongly with the military wisdom of bombing Iraq: Major-General (ret.) Lewis MacKenzie, the first United Nations Peacekeeping Forces commander in Sarajevo in 1992, and Commander Jim Allen, the Chief of Staff of the UN peacekeeping forces in the Mid-East in 1990. (Even U.S. Gen. Norman Schwarzkopf expressed serious doubts about the military wisdom of such an air attack.) And yet Canada's politicians proceeded to support the threatened bombing. Lewis MacKenzie expressed concern about unnecessarily "killing more people."

Prime Minister Chrétien's concern, on the other hand, was with "cleaning up that mess" in Iraq. But two of his top military men were saying it would not work. Was this an honest attempt to clean up a mess, or was it a politically motivated decision? Chrétien was well aware that to say no to the U.S. would have serious economic consequences—especially now that we are so tightly connected through NAFTA.

As Richard Sanders, coordinator of the *Coalition to Oppose the Arms Trade*, noted a short while ago: "Canada's military exports [to the U.S. have never] been stopped, or even reduced, because the U.S. has armed, financed, trained and equipped the combatants in coups against democratically elected governments, undermined and rigged elections, assassinated (or tried to assassinate) scores of foreign leaders, and propped up ruthless dictators who offered U.S. corporations union-free and low-wage factories and cheap access to their countries' natural resources."

Canada is the 13th largest military spender in the world, placing us in the top ten percent of the more than 180 states around the world. As Ron Dart, Professor at the University College of the Fraser Valley in British Columbia, notes, "Canada's military budget is larger than the military budget of all the countries of South America combined. Our $12 billion annual military budget is more than twice as large as the entire annual peacekeeping budget of the United Nations. The department of war—a.k.a. Department of National Defense (DND)—only spends 5.8 percent of its budget on peacekeeping." The federal government spends 600 percent more on war than on affordable housing, according to the Ontario group *Homes Not Bombs*.

Industry Canada hands out millions of dollars of our tax money to multinationals involved in the business of war. Some of their products are deemed "civilian," even though they can be used for military purposes. There is no official mechanism to determine whether commercial hardware and components from Canada end up in the hands of dictators.

Was liberating Kuwait from Iraq really the mess Chrétien was concerned about? Then "Why," asks Professor Dart, "have we done nothing about liberating the Kurd and Marsh Arabs in Iraq from Hussein, the Tibetans from the Chinese, the East Timorese-Achech from the Indonesians, the Kurdish people from Turkey, the Mayans from Guatemala?"

The Liberal government did not talk about the innocent people who would be massacred in the event of renewed bombing, nor about the 5,000 Iraqi children under five dying each month as a result of UN sanctions. More people have been killed from sanctions than from the 88,500 tons of bombs that were dropped on Iraq during the Gulf War. More Iraqi children have died as a result of sanctions than the combined toll of two atomic bombs on Japan and the recent scourge of ethnic cleansing in the former Yugoslavia. This is a silent holocaust in the name of the UN which is similar in number to those killed by the dictator Pol Pot in the genocide in Cambodia.

John Dear put it this way after a visit to Iraq: "World War Two's second worst atrocity (after the Holocaust) was the siege of Leningrad. It caused over a million civilian deaths—more than the bombings on Hiroshima, Nagasaki, Hamburg, Cologne and Coventry put together. Most of them particularly horrible deaths from malnutrition and disease. Most of them children, who are particularly susceptible. The German commander leading that siege was put on trial at Nuremburg as a war criminal. The United Nations—no fan of Saddam Hussein—now reports…the same numbers and types of deaths [in Iraq] as in the siege of Leningrad."

Dear further commented on the use of sanctions as an instrument of war. "Once before, sanctions starved a people to try to coerce their government. After the Armistice had ended World War One, a naval blockade kept food and medicine from Germany to try to force acceptance of the harsh Treaty of Versailles. This became a key reason why so many Germans turned to Hitler. And now, much worse hunger and death are supposed to bring human leadership and democracy to

Iraq." A proper nonviolent application of sanctions would have focussed on military products—not on the weak and powerless.

In a February 11, 1998 CBC radio report, Retired Commander Jim Allen declared, "Chrétien hasn't thought this through…There are all kinds of ramifications to using military action to no purpose…We are just a doormat." Unusually, even some Liberal Members of Parliament publicly opposed their own government's decision. "Instead of waging war again, we should find ways to drive a wedge between the population and the military leadership. Why penalize the civilian population?… Why not abandon the fruitless imposition of sanctions?" asserted Liberal MP Charles Caccia. Alexa McDonough, leader of the NDP (which still clings to its own Left version of the Just War doctrine) noted that "It is estimated by the Food and Agriculture Organization of the United Nations that one child dies every 10 minutes today in Iraq as a result of those sanctions."

Democracy?
Without a UN mandate, the U.S.—still refusing to pay its full share of UN expenses—prepared to bomb Iraq. Then President Clinton called Canada's prime minister for moral backing. Chrétien committed military support before full parliamentary debate. Democracy?

U.S., British and Canadian politicians claimed to want to punish Hussein because he was defying UN resolutions. Then why do they allow Israel to defy UN resolutions and possess nuclear weapons? This is a concern for democracy?

The U.S. military rightly claims that Hussein is guilty of violating other nations. It is important to expose these violations. But what about the U.S. government? The U.S. *School of the Americas (SOA)* trains 900–2,000 soldiers a year from Latin America and the Caribbean to make war on their own peoples. Recent revelations show that the SOA actively teaches torture techniques. U.S. Catholic priest Roy Bourgeois and others have tried to shut down this "School of Assassins"—which has trained officers who are responsible for some of the worst atrocities in Latin America since it was founded in 1946. This is not violating other nations? Should not a UN inspection team be allowed free access to the SOA? Should not Iraqi inspectors join others in demanding the truth? Thousands of people have been arrested simply for attempting to deliver petitions with more than 100,000 signatures calling for the closing of the U.S. Army School of the Americas.

The SOA gets $18.4 million of U.S. taxpayers' money. The Fellowship of Reconciliation-USA (FOR-USA) is a faith-based network committed to active nonviolence—comprised of such groups as the Catholic Peace Fellowship, the Jewish Peace Fellowship and the Muslim Peace Fellowship. It has a budget of $1,681,398—nine percent of the SOA's budget. The FOR gets nothing from the U.S. government.

The SOA's position is consistent: if you are going to maintain the Institution of War abroad, you *do* need to maintain—and therefore refine and teach—the military skill of torture. There are an estimated 5,000,000 torture victims in the world. There are about 200 centres in the world which help to heal victims of torture. That's an average of 25,000 people per centre. Canada, one of the wealthiest countries in the world, gives a shameful $18,000 to the UN for these victims—less than most countries give.

"Weapons of mass destruction…"
Within four weeks of taking office as President of the United States of America, George W. Bush authorized the bombing of Iraq: "Our intention is to make sure that the world is as peaceful as possible. We are going to watch very carefully as to whether or not (Saddam) develops weapons of mass destruction.

Who is the U.S. to accuse other nations of having weapons of mass destruction when its arsenal exceeds anything the world has ever seen? Yes, Iraq should not have weapons of mass destruction, nor should the U.S., Britain, Israel, France and all other countries who stockpile nuclear weapons. Nor should Canada hypocritically benefit from supporting its allies' continuing possession of nuclear weapons and from its refusal to advocate any change to NATO's nuclear policy. In December 1996 and 1997, a majority of states in the UN General Assembly called upon all states to commence multilateral negotiations leading to an early conclusion of a nuclear weapons convention to abolish nuclear weapons. Canada voted against these resolutions. How many Canadians know or care? It does not fit our cherished myth of Canada as peacemaker.

War and the rule of wealth
At the turn of the 20th century, the whole British war fleet, then the biggest in the world, converted from coal to oil power. Since then, oil has been essential for the military. And what is essential for the military becomes essential for everything else, regardless of the efficiency of other decentralized sources of power such as wind and sun.

Iraq has the second largest known oil reserve in the world. As long as the U.S. has a bloated military budget to feed, it will continue to kill for its oil interests. The U.S. military is the number one consumer of oil in the world. In fact, the U.S. is addicted to oil. In the U.S., when a baby born today reaches age 75, he or she will have used 3,375 barrels of oil. Each year 180 million gallons of motor oil are sent to landfills—the equivalent of 16 Exxon Valdez spills. Though 90 percent of the world's six billion people do not own a car, 90 percent of U.S. citizens have at least one car. If a car lasts 100,000 miles, it will dump nearly 35 tons of carbon dioxide into the air. As a world we pump over a ton of carbon dioxide into the atmosphere every year for every man, woman and child alive. Every year, 16,000 Canadians die prematurely from the effects of air pollutants.

Canada's largest independent oil and gas company, Talisman Energy of Calgary, is developing oil in Sudan where millions have been killed in a civil war since 1983. There are about 15,000 Sudanese held as slaves. Profiteering, slavery and war. Oil and warmaking go together today as gold and warmaking did in Christopher Columbus' time. As historian John Bacher put it in his book *Petrotyranny*, "Warrior dictators in the Middle East need not fear taxpayer revolt. Their military schemes are founded on their control over oil."

Rather than develop a truly independent vision of peacemaking, the Canadian government timidly acquiesces to the U.S. military's dictates. There are over 100,000 people in Canada's military (active, reserve and civil defense). Imagine 100,000 people—paid to develop and maintain, on a daily basis, serious nonviolent civilian-based defence (CBD). Then we might honestly claim to have a Department of National Defence.

Besides civilian-based defence, there is also the work of violence reduction by groups such as the Christian Peacemaker Teams (CPT). CPT sends teams of trained peacemakers into situations of violent conflict and areas of militarization to support local efforts for nonviolent solutions. CPT is a project of the Church of the Brethren, General Conference

Mennonite, Mennonite Church congregations and Friends (Quakers) United Meeting—the three peace churches. Where are the mainline churches in this urgent work? The combined membership of the mainline churches in Canada is 20 million. In North America it is 330 million; worldwide it represents 1.9 billion people. Here are such vast spiritual and financial resources that are **not** put at the disposal of real peacemaking, while the church's tax money ends up supporting, by default or by choice, only one institution in times of international crisis: the military.

Very soon after the 1991 Gulf War, five Canadian government ministers toured the Middle East region in an effort to help boost Canadian arms sales, especially in Kuwait. Had the blood even dried yet? The tears of widows and orphans certainly hadn't. About 75 percent of Canada's military industrial production is exported to about 60 countries that are mostly in what is called the "developing world." As Randolph Bournes, a U.S. World War I pacifist, once put it, "War is the health of the State." The mainline churches pray for peace but work, organize, risk and pay for war—and reap the benefits.

To critique militarism without critiquing the economy is unrealistic. But to critique the economy without critiquing the daily expenditure of militarism is even more unrealistic. (Too many people still don't know the true spelling of *militarism*: *millitari$m*.) All the wealthy countries, including Canada, live off war, either through the actual fighting of wars to expand our interests, or more commonly, by the ongoing threat of war—for which we need a permanent war economy: the research, design, manufacture, promotion, sale and maintenance of weapons systems. All this has long been normal. But simply because we are *used* to evil doesn't make it acceptable. We are used to building our "progress" and our "prosperity" on brutal militarism. This does not make it right. As long as slavery was sanctioned by law and was not resisted, capitalism took full advantage of it. Until there is what Martin Luther King Jr. called a "revolution of values," we will continue to have governments that are ideologically driven by a brutal "common sense revolution" for the rich. As University of Toronto Professor Emeritus Ursula Franklin puts it: "War needs two things—an enemy and money."

Those who critique the economy from an alternative position need to be relentless in making the connections between militarism and poverty; between militarism and corporate globalization. A good example is the *Economic Justice Report* of March 1998, put out by the Ecumenical

Coalition on Economic Justice (ECEJ). Here, ECEJ shows how the U.S. and the other countries involved in the FTAA are trying to fight against most government subsidized enterprises which are integral to the common good, such as the CBC, Canada Post and Via Rail. Meanwhile, the report shows, "The United States is seeking a sweeping exemption for its huge, highly-subsidized, military industrial complex."

The feminist economist Marilyn Waring has exposed how the international system of economic measurement used by banks and corporations accounts only for cash-generating activities. The Toronto feminist and environmentalist, Dorothy Goldin Rosenberg, had this to say in her review of Waring's book *If Women Counted: A New Feminist Economics*:

> A nation's annual budget should reflect real wealth. It should enable us to answer such questions as: Who does the work—paid and unpaid—and where is it done? What is the position of the children and the aged? Who is not housed adequately? Who has the poorest health? What changes have occurred in the water and air quality, and why? Where does pollution exist? What causes it, and what are the health costs? What national resources have been harvested or conserved? Who carries the burden of caring for others? What is the scope of subsistence production and what are the nutritional results?

There is a deep, inextricable connection between war and poverty. There is a deep, inextricable connection between perpetual war and perpetual poverty. A national housing strategy for Canada would cost about $2 billion a year. The military spends $10 billion on weapons. Which expenditure builds real, lasting security? Is the agenda really about security?

In Canada, half of all the families hold 94 percent of all the wealth. The other half is left with six percent. The richest ten percent have a net worth of $703,500, while the poorest ten percent have a negative worth of minus $2,100. Canada's CEOs were paid an average of $2,654,116 in 1995, nearly 90 times the average wage of working Canadians at $29,835. We are developing an economic culture more and more similar to that of the U.S., where Bill Gates, Warren Buffett and the John Walton family

(Walmart) have greater combined assets than the poorest 100 million U.S. citizens: $94 billion versus $90 billion.

I recently heard a young person committed to confronting the globalization of wealth at the 2001 Summit of the Americas in Québec City say, "The world has changed. We've become a commodity." People have always been a commodity for militarism and its economy. It's just that now, more and more comfortable Canadians are actually feeling it. In resisting corporate power, they will necessarily confront its military might. Will the decision to resist "nonviolently" remain a merely pragmatic choice of tactics? Or will it lead to a discovery of nonviolent resistance as the *other force*?

I remember the arrogance of Litton Systems, when it declared in the eighties, "We have sold to Chile when the U.S. was against selling to Chile. We sold to Argentina and all those places. We would sell to Libya and Iraq if they required something." It is crucial that we not separate the issue of the globalization of the economy from its necessary militarism. The two are utterly inseparable. "The evils of racism, economic exploitation and militarism are all tied together...you can't really get rid of one without getting rid of the others," declared Martin Luther King Jr. The recent anti-globalization demonstrations in Seattle and Québec City expose yet again the military power behind those in possession of the means of wealth.

The church and sister water: reclaiming our ancient spiritual wisdom

In a letter from Birmingham Jail, Martin Luther King Jr. wrote, "I have been disappointed with the church. I do not say this as one of those negative critics who can always find something wrong with the church. I say this as a minister of the gospel, who loves the church; who has been nurtured in its bosom; who has been sustained by its spiritual blessings; and who will remain true to it as long as the cord of life shall lengthen."

At the time of the threatened bombing of Iraq, our faith and resistance group (mentioned above) reflected on its own disappointment with the church:

> We long for the church community to become its true self'
> to reclaim a vision of God's commonwealth for all, not just
> the wealthy and militarily powerful; a vision of power as free,

radical service; a vision of cooperation and reconciliation rather than brutal, wasteful competition and victory. The globalization of greed and its necessary militarism is destroying this vision while causing the suffering of countless people and violating the Earth. In order to more fully join with others in resisting the force of greed and destruction, we need to reclaim the early church community's understanding of the other force—the soul force we now call "nonviolence." The full renunciation of all war is a necessary first step towards becoming more fully the Beloved Community.

The whole of the *Cross and Sword* witness and trial was a cry for us to reclaim our most ancient radical spiritual wisdom as church—especially in relation to the mystery of love of enemies. As the late bishop of Gatineau-Hull, Adolphe Proulx stated, we "must be able to read again the gospels and to embrace the attitude of the first Christians who rejected war, even if their lives were endangered."

During a retreat I facilitated, a thoughtful and committed Catholic asked why it was that the pope could renounce capital punishment but not war. He knew better than most people that even though John Paul II had courageously denounced the atrocities of war, he never fully renounced the Institution of War itself. The pope symbolizes the position of all the mainstream church leaders, whether they lean to the right or to the left of the centre. Recently I was asked to address a community of Cistercian monks on gospel nonviolence. One of them said that he felt that the pope was "on the verge of renouncing war itself." Why is it taking so long for church leaders to make that declaration of faith? Among all the complex reasons, I see three that are central: centuries of a culture of justified war; a consequent erosion of faith in God's power in the face of great danger or evil; and a seriously flawed spirituality that leaves Christians incapable of integrating Holy Disobedience with Holy Obedience.

Centuries of justified war
Years ago, while John Paul II was telling the priests of Latin America not to become involved in politics, he was at the same time canonizing two Polish priests who had engaged in an armed conflict against the Czarists. He claimed that their armed struggle had been part of their

sanctity. Nationalism still maims our faith as Christians. Nationalism is still one of the excuses for declaring some wars (ours!) as being justified. Only the "common security" that some churches are calling for can free us of the deadly myths of "national security."

Beyond the public leadership of the church, more disturbing to me is the effect that centuries of the normalization of war has had on ordinary Christians who otherwise exhibit great spiritual wisdom. Recently a seasoned member of a religious community who works with the poor asked whether war was "more important than issues like poverty or the refugee crisis." The question fails to recognize that the issues are simply and utterly inseparable. The illusion that war is "over there" or "less immediate" stunts our capacity to fully resist poverty or the plight of refugees.

In Canada, where our extreme relative wealth and personal safety render us almost oblivious to the ravages of war, maybe it is only by living the mystery of the One Body more fully that we will cease to divorce militarism from issues such as environmental degradation, globalization of greed and poverty.

"At this point in our history we have a choice: to be partners in the reign of justice or dealers in the reign of death," declared Bishop Thomas Gumbleton. We have indeed become dealers of death. After centuries of sanctioned warfare, we also have become addicted to the 'benefits' of its brutal economy.

In accepting an honourary degree from Trinity College at the University of Toronto in February 2000, Desmond Tutu wondered out loud what would happen if the healthy, functional ethics of a supportive family were applied to the nations of this small world, "We would not spend such obscene amounts in our budgets of death and destruction, called defense spending, when a small fraction of those budgets would ensure that our sisters and brothers everywhere would have clean water, enough to eat, adequate health care, a good education and a secure home environment." In a letter to Pakistani ruler Pervez Musharraf, dated May 25, 2001, Indian Prime Minister Atal Behari Vajpayee stated: "Our common enemy is poverty. For the welfare of our peoples, there is no other recourse but a pursuit of the path of reconciliation…We have to pick up the threads again." Even states that still cling to the Institution of War, like India and Pakistan, must at some point confront the deadly cost of this addictive system. As Tutu has said elsewhere, "Without forgiveness, there is no future."

We have become dealers, pushers of death. In Burma, it is heroin which keeps the generals in power. In the U.S., Colonel Oliver North used $14 million from drugs to finance arms sales. These are symbols of war as addiction.

A child is sent to the store to buy medicine for a seriously ill mother. Instead he buys candy for himself. Would we say such dysfunction is cute? Both for the child's and the mother's sake we would confront the situation. As a people, we need to grow up, face our addictions and make hard choices. We have a very sick culture to tend to.

The most fascinating part of the story of the rich young man who asked Jesus how to live life fully is that, even though he chose to keep all his wealth—his addiction—*he did not go away happy*. He chose his addiction over the freedom of Christ. *And went away sad*. He rejected Christ's fullness of life. By clinging to our 'right' to the Sword, we reject the mystery of love of enemy. Rejecting the mystery of love of enemy is rejecting Christ. Has it made us happy, secure?

A choice between two forces
For most Christians—and other people of faith—nonviolence may be good; it may be very good; it may even be considered urgent. But almost never is it understood as being a *force—the force of love*. Literally a force. Nonviolence is what I call simply "the other force." There are two forces in the world. We must make a *choice*.

The great lie of the Sword on the Cross is that it presents the Sword as the ultimate force needed to confront serious injustice or violence. The consequent lie is that we need not make a *choice*: we can have both the Cross and the Sword.

Over a decade ago the Canadian Religious Conference officially declared that *justice* was a constitutive element of its vision. In June 2000, the 300 leaders of Canada's religious communities invited me to their bi-annual conference to probe gospel nonviolence. The question I put before them was "*With which force* will we as a church community do the work of justice?" I proposed that just as justice had been declared *constitutive*, so gospel nonviolence should be considered a *constitutive* part of the work for justice.

With which force? It is crucial that we stop trivializing nonviolence and refuse the false choice of "nonviolence or force." The true choice is between the force of hatred/violence and the force of love we call "nonviolence." Addressing the problem of violence, the moderator of the World Council of Churches' Central Committee was quoted in the March 2001 issue of the *Anglican Journal*: "We do not judge those for whom, in extreme situations, when hope for justice and dignity has disappeared, the use of force as a last resort may become necessary." No! Force must be used *immediately*, not as a last resort, when we are confronted with serious injustice: the soul force of nonviolent resistance, with its many powerful tools. This force must be used immediately, not as a last resort, against the abuses of power by the Iraqi and U.S. military regimes.

One way to probe this further is to compare the two forces in their organized states:

(1) The organized force of violence
(e.g. socially sanctioned armies or illegal guerilla groups)
(2) The organized force of nonviolence
(e.g. the legal U.S. civil rights movement, or the village of Le Chambon's illegal resistance to the Nazis, or the Philippine people's nonviolent overthrow of the Marcos military dictatorship)

- Where one needs *weapons*, the other depends on the powerful *tools* of active nonviolence (public education; conflict transformation; demonstrations; noncooperation; intervention; alternatives).
- Where one depends on a rigid *hierarchy* of authority, the other relies on the indestructible trust of genuine *community and leadership*.
- Where one depends on *giving and following orders*, the other lives the mystery of *obedience*, which is the deepest possible listening to one another—including the enemy.
- And finally, where one aims for *victory* over individuals or groups, the other's constant goal is *reconciliation*.

It has taken me a long time to understand just how pervasively the culture of victory, winning and competition has poisoned us. I have just begun to see how few people do the sometimes hard, dangerous and frightening spiritual work of renouncing the culture of victory.

A CHOICE BETWEEN TWO FORCES	
The organized force of violence	**The organized force of nonviolence**
Weapons	Tools
Hierarchy	Community
Orders: giving and following	Obedience: deepest possible listening
Victory	Reconciliation

Too many people who publicly profess to believe in reconciliation still secretly cling to the myth of victory as "more exciting" than reconciliation—just as competition is seen as "more exciting" than cooperation. For too many people, reconciliation may be the morally proper thing to aim for, but it is not exciting. The BOOM and BANG of violence titillates and intoxicates. (I was disturbed to see how many people allowed themselves to watch day after day the repulsive Gulf War visual propaganda, which reduced the mass destruction and murder to bright explosions on the television screen. It reminded me of the Romans passively watching slaughter as entertainment.)

I believe that until we confront and renounce the real power which victory has over us we only approach reconciliation as a moral duty and can never be physically, mentally, emotionally and spiritually stimulated by its depth and breadth.

Part of the problem is that, in a culture that props up this myth of victory-as-excitement, we hear too few of the powerful stories of reconciliation. Stanley W. Green, originally from South Africa, now President of the U.S. Mennonite Board of Missions, told the story of an elderly South African woman who had suffered terrible losses at the hands of a brutal murderer.

She stood in an emotionally charged courtroom, listening to a group of white police officers acknowledge the atrocities they had perpetrated in the name of apartheid. Officer van de Broek acknowledged his personal responsibility in the death of her son. Along with others, van de Broek shot her 18-year-old son at point-blank range. The group partied while they burned his body, turning it over and over on the fire until it was completely reduced to ashes. Eight years later, van de Broek and others arrived to collect her husband. A few years later, shortly after midnight, van de Broek again appeared and took the woman to a place beside a river. On a woodpile her husband lay bound. They forced her to watch as they poured gasoline over his body and ignited the flames that consumed his body. The last words she heard him say were, "Forgive them." Now, van de Broek stood before her awaiting judgment. Vengeance seemed inevitable. The Truth and Reconciliation Commission officers asked her what she wanted. "I want three things," she said calmly. "I want Mr. Van de Broek to take me to the place where they burned my husband's body. I would like to gather up the dust and give him a decent burial. Second, Mr. Van de Broek took all my family away from me and I still have a lot of love to give. Twice a month, I would like for him to come to the ghetto and spend a day with me so I can be a mother to him. Third, I would like Mr. Van de Broek to know that he is forgiven by God, and that I forgive him, too. And, I would like someone to come and lead me by the hand to where Mr. Van de Broek is, so that I can embrace him and he can know my forgiveness is real." As they led the elderly woman across the silent courtroom, van de Broek fainted, overwhelmed. In the courtroom, someone began singing "Amazing Grace." Gradually, others joined in until, finally, everyone there was singing the familiar hymn.

Is the story of victory really more exciting than the story of reconciliation? Could we not give up a few Rambo movies and use our massive artistic resources to tell the stories of reconciliation to a spiritually starved culture? A spiritually healthy culture would expose the lie that reconciliation is only for elders—who have lost the taste for competition and victory. In a spiritually healthy culture, youth would feel the challenge and excitement of cooperation and reconciliation.

"Liberation means that the oppressed are freed from being oppressed and the oppressors are freed from being oppressors," reflected Desmond Tutu.

NATO generals have their own definition of freedom and power. They talk of "hard power" and "soft power." Soft power is that moral, nonviolent stuff that aims for reconciliation, which is usually trivialized and rarely given any serious resources. When the generals determine that what they call soft power doesn't 'work,' they ask the "well-intentioned people" to step aside and let hard power take over—usually expressed as bombing. Hard power, we are assured, really works.

Historian William Blum compiled a list of the countries the U.S. has bombed (hard power) since the end of World War II; China 1945–46; Korea 1950–53; China 1950–53; Guatemala 1954; Indonesia 1958; Cuba 1959–60; Guatemala 1967–69; Cambodia 1969–70; Grenada 1983; Libya 1986; El Salvador 1980s; Nicaragua 1980s; Panama 1989; Iraq 1991–2001; Sudan 1998; Afghanistan 1998; Yugoslavia 1999; Afghanistan 2001. As to the success of this hard power we might ask in how many of these instances did a democratic government, respectful of human rights, occur as a direct result? Not a single one.

Canadians believe in this hard power versus soft power myth. We are making ourselves spiritually weak by relying on "hard power." Our armed forces could **never** defend us against our most likely attacker—the only country which has attacked us in the past—the U.S. we need to become stronger, less passively dependent on expensive high-tech "hard power" and its pushers. We need the fullest possible participation of the people for collective cooperation with the common good and collective noncooperation with all internal or foreign domination. This requires serious spiritual discipline and training for Civilian Nonviolent Defence, whose final goal is lasting reconciliation, not mere victory of the Sword.

True sovereignty and full liberation for any people cannot be founded on the false power of the Sword. The depth and the breadth of reconciliation are the depth and breadth of freedom.

Holy obedience, holy disobedience
Church people rightly respond to the endless stream of war refugees. I have taken refugees into my home on a number of occasions. There is no question that we need to respond to the refugee crisis. But as long as we do not *at the same time* publicly denounce the very Institution of War, the foundation for all our works of charity and mercy is utterly false. And the stream of suffering sisters and brothers will continue to swell. Wars rage in approximately one-fifth of the countries of the world, causing a flood of refugees whose numbers are close to the population of Canada! We do not fully love our refugee sisters and brothers unless we commit ourselves to addressing the root causes of their plight. To paraphrase Dom Helder Camara: "When I help refugees, they call me a saint. When I ask why we don't publicly renounce the very Institution of War that creates this flood of refugees, they call me an Idealist."

Refugees are an inevitable part of warfare. The United Nations sets a minimum standard for refugee camps. It is not surprising to me that some of my own wealthy city's emergency shelters for the homeless do not meet those basic standards: the minimal care of refugees is a necessary part of the maintenance of the sacred Institution of War. The homeless are not directly part of that visible face of war and so there is not the same public pressure on governments to offer them equal resources.

Religious people are generally good at performing the works of mercy, but not at resisting the works of war. People of faith obey the good but are rarely as willing to disobey evil. We say YES, but are afraid to say the consequent NO. It is not enough, by any measure of faith, to just be against war, to regret it or to be repulsed by it. It is not even enough to know we would never agree to go to war. We need to publicly express our renunciation and our resistance.

How many people really believe that genuine disobedience is literally as holy as genuine obedience? We need to practice obedience by refusing to follow orders. We need to teach our children to disobey by teaching them the difference between genuine obedience and following orders. A parent once confessed to me that he was seriously tempted to send his son into the army "to learn discipline." I told him that what his son would learn was how to follow orders—a passive, fake discipline.

Mere revulsion is not renunciation—let alone resistance
Echoing Cicero's insight that "infinite money" (i.e. taxation) is essential for war, General Electric's president, Charles Wilson, noted in 1944, "The revulsion against war not too long hence will be an almost insuperable obstacle for us to overcome. For that reason, I am convinced that we must begin now to set the machinery in motion for a *permanent war economy*." We have been living in a permanent war economy ever since.

Many in the Christian churches experience "revulsion" at the thought of a messy war in the Middle East—or elsewhere. Yet revulsion is not renunciation or conversion, nor is it resistance.

Every group wants the perfect war: the perfect Left war, the perfect Right war and the perfect Religious war. Personally, I have more respect for the consistency of the U.S. military leader who, when confronted with people's revulsion at the burying alive of escaping, terrified Iraqi boys/soldiers in the desert, bluntly stated that there is no neat way to make war. There simply isn't. There is no war without massive abuse of one kind of another.

Church leaders make pronouncements about individual wars. But until we renounce, denounce and resist War itself, all our declarations about individual wars, however dramatic, hold no moral power anymore, especially for young people. "Facta, non verba!"—Deeds, not words!

Renunciation is not passive. It is rooted in the living Spirit of God. Renunciation is not mere moral dutifulness, nor mere avoidance of sin. Renunciation makes genuine repentance possible. You cannot repent of rape unless you renounce rape. Renunciation is a radical insistence on "life to the fullest," as Christ announced God's presence. The very moment of renunciation is the beginning of freedom. Renunciation is not merely a faint hope—nor even the strong conviction—that something better might happen—nor even the strong conviction—that something better might happen—*in the future*. The very act of renunciation is a radical act of liberation—*in the present moment*. The moment a male truly renounces rape, he is changed. The moment a church body truly renounces War, it is transformed.

Just as we are afraid of freedom, we are afraid of the real costs of renouncing war: pressure on our financial resources; the testing of our relationships; the possibility of being marginalized, even ridiculed.

Without a radical renunciation of the very Institution of War, we are left reacting helplessly to the relentless lurching of the global war machine. A *Globe and Mail* editorial (July 14, 1998) entitled "Peace and Justice" stated, "The Nuremberg and Tokyo Tribunals after the Second World War set a precedent for dealing with atrocities committed *under the guise of war.*" War itself is an atrocity! Of course, any limit to the atrocity of war is to be welcomed. But the atrocity of war remains.

As a rare treat, I recently went with my co-worker, Jim, and his wife, Mary Eileen, to a great benefit concert promoting a "land-mine-free world." I thoroughly relished the music of Bruce Cockburn, John Prine and Emmylou Harris. At one point in the evening we heard a moving talk by a veteran of the Vietnamese War, an intensely dedicated man in a wheelchair. He and his group were doing exciting things for the healing of victims of land mines. Yet at one point in his talk he essentially echoed the *Globe and Mail's* position: protecting the necessary Institution of War from "atrocities"—in this case land mines. He talked about how mines were the only weapons left behind in warfare. That was why they were so despicable, he told us.

The only weapons left behind? This is a dangerous view of war. Try telling that to the parents of babies seriously deformed by the effects of Depleted Uranium. Try telling that to the farmers whose lungs and fields are poisoned with defoliants. Try telling that to the 300,000 child soldiers who are indoctrinated and often provided with drugs. Try telling that to the parents of the two million child soldiers who have been killed around the world. Try telling that to the sex slaves of the world's wars. Try telling that to the 12 million children left homeless because of war; the over 1 million orphaned or separated from parents; the 10 million psychologically traumatized. Whether hardware or not, they are all lasting 'weapons' of war. They are *all* left behind. They all degrade. They all maim.

I deeply honour the great work of this veteran. But I have a moral responsibility to cry out and say: it is War that is the atrocity! According to *Project Ploughshares*, over the course of the 20th century, the civilian portion of war-related deaths has vastly increased, climbing from ten percent at its dawn, to less than 50 per cent in the years up to 1950, to over 90 per cent in the 1990s.

I fully understand the U.S. military's refusal to sign the treaty banning land mines. If you are to fight wars—especially if the burden of protecting the "free world" rests on you—you need the fullest possible arsenal. The U.S. position is logical, even though it is based on a profoundly sick premise. And it is less hypocritical than Canada's position: if the Canadian state actually had to fight its own wars and do its own threatening of nations, rather than depend on the massive U.S. nuclear war machine, I'm convinced we would not be banning land mines so easily. Or have we become so blind that we think of our own warmaking as more "humane"? Was Canada's bombing of Iraqi children, women and men more "humane" that that of the U.S.?

Renouncing war is not renouncing power. It is renouncing false power. It is renouncing the abuse of power. Renunciation is about the *transformation of power*, not merely the transfer of power: transforming, for example, the *power over* of rape into the *power with* of mutual respect and mutual risk-taking resistance to violence against women. At the very moment of renouncing false power, we enter into the life-giving power of love, which we name nonviolence. We become immediately engaged in its exploration.

Born, not again, but over and over: conversion
"You need a conversion to commit yourself to nonviolence. It is not something you reach by logic or force of arguments." The profound truth of this simple observation by Bishop Thomas Gumbleton is foundational to an understanding of nonviolence as the force of love that includes love of enemy. No book, no retreat can convert us to nonviolence. We have to open a deep space for grace to move in our lives. We have to allow Christ to fully confront our deepest fears and our greatest yearnings.

Do not most of us yearn for peace? Our yearning must be turned into the embodied prayer of resistance. The prayer of resistance can lead us to conversion to the life-giving mystery of love of enemy. Love of enemy—within and without—exposes our fears. In all cultures, genuine resistance born of love is automatically very fearful and costly. The pain is the pain of birthing a new culture. As Hildegard Goss-Mayr of the International Fellowship of Reconciliation (IFOR) put it so eloquently: "We must become midwives, in order to give birth to this liberating force which already exists in all peoples."

Dying, not once, but over and over: seed
When we choose the Sword over the Cross (or make them interchangeable), we act as if Christ said "I am come that they may have safety and have it more abundantly." Christ does not offer a guarantee of physical survival, but rather life in its fullest.

Life is filled with conflict and death. We are confronted with conflict and death daily. Christ invites us to come to terms with conflict and death as part of life. "Unless the seed die, it remains alone." Learning to face "Sister Bodily Death" teaches us to honour the sacredness of life and to renounce the blasphemy of killing. We can never be free until we go beyond the fear of all deaths, whatever they might be. Freedom from fear is freedom from violence. A church this free would be a church capable of offering great, indestructible joy to the world.

A Cry of Love
A powerful symbol of hope comes to us in a group of 20th century monks from the same community as Bernard of Clairvaux, the Cistercians, more popularly known as Trappists. These particular monks lived in Tibhirine, Algeria. They lived among Muslims as brothers. As contemplatives, they shared their lives with the poor in their neighbourhood. Their vow of stability bore fruit as a deep mutual love grew between them and their neighbours. When their lives were threatened by fundamentalist extremists, they refused to leave. On the night of March 26, 1996, seven of them were abducted by men with guns. On May 21, when their lives were no longer useful as international bargaining tools, their throats were slit.

One of the murdered monks was Christian de Chergé, prior of the Tibhirine monastery. His testament is a stunning monument to the powerful and lifegiving mystery of love of enemy. Months before his assassination, aware of the risks that his community was taking in choosing to stay with their neighbours and friends, Christian had written:

> It if should happen one day—and it could be today—that I become a victim of the terrorism which now seems ready to encompass all the foreigners living in Algeria, I would like my community, my Church, my family to remember that my life was *given* to God and to this country...I would like them to be able to associate this death with so many other

equally violent ones that have been allowed to fall into the indifference of anonymity. My life has no more value than any other. Nor any less value…I should like, when the time comes, to have a space of lucidity which would enable me to beg forgiveness of God and of my brothers and sisters in the human family, and at the same time to forgive will all my heart the one who would strike me down. I could not desire such a death. It seems important to state this…In this *thank you* where all is said for everything in my life from now on, I certainly include you, friends of yesterday and today, and you, O my friends of this place, besides my mother and my father, my sisters and my brothers and their families, the hundredfold given as he had promised! *And you, too, my last minute friend, who would not have known what you were doing, yes, for you too, I say this thank you and this "A-DIEU"—to commend you to the God in whose face I see yours…Amen! Inshallah!*

On July 5, 1830, the French military invaded Algeria, conquered it and annexed its territory to France. Out of that victory came decades of fear, hatred, torture and assassinations. As a Frenchman, Christian's life, freely *given* in love for the people of Algeria, long before it was taken, witnessed to the possibility of reconciliation and the breaking of that degrading cycle of violence.

Three years before his assassination, Christian had encountered another band of armed revolutionaries who had come to the monastery. At about nine o'clock on Christmas Eve, 1993, Christian confronted the armed men with these words: "This is a house of peace; no one has every entered here with arms. If you want to discuss with us, come in, but leave your arms outside."

Christian and his six brother monks had their throats slit. Yet their cry of love still resounds and confronts our fear. As a faith community, we betray their martyrdom unless their cry becomes the cry of the entire church before the whole world: This is a house of peace! Come in, but without the weapons of fear, greed and hatred!

The sword at the centre of the cross is the clearest symbol of the Just War teachings of the mainline churches. This war memorial is located at St. Paul's Anglican Church, Bloor Street, Toronto, the Garrison Church of the Queen's Own Rifles Regiment.

2 Cross and ploughshare or cross and sword?

A brief history of the public witness

"Garrison Church"

> St. Paul's Anglican Church, Bloor Street, has been asked by a small group of "concerned Christians" to alter the appearance of the war memorial located on its property at 227 Bloor Street East. St. Paul's is the Garrison Church of The Queen's Own Rifles Regiment, who erected a monument in 1931 in memory of its members who had lost their lives while serving in its ranks.

So began a May 3, 1998 public notice, circulated by the Corporation of St. Paul's (rector and wardens) after a meeting we had had with them where we presented our request. They received us hospitably. Both sides listened to each other. Precisely put, our request was to come to terms with the social implications of Christ's call to love our enemies and to publicly renounce the false teaching of the Just War. As a symbol of that renunciation, we were requesting that the sword be carefully taken off the cross, transformed into a ploughshare, and returned to the cross as a public sign of that renunciation.

The public notice from St. Paul's Corporation continued:

The monument, known as the Cross of Sacrifice, is a simple granite cross, with a sword at rest upon it. Sixty-seven years ago, the memorial was dedicated to the Glory of God, in the presence of the Queen's Own Rifles, by the Rector of St. Paul's, the Rev. Canon Henry J. Cody. Today, it is a visible reminder of the 1,730 members of the Queen's Own Rifles who lost their lives in its service.

With the endorsement of the parish leadership and the Queen's Own Rifles Regiment, the Corporation will not undertake any modification to the Cross of Sacrifice. St. Paul's remains deeply committed to Jesus Christ, the Prince of Peace and to the proclamation of His Gospel. The sword on the Cross of Sacrifice stands at rest, in the shadow of the almighty Cross of Christ. The people of St. Paul's Bloor Street join in the prayers for peace, and are thankful for the freedom to worship God and to make the Gospel of Jesus Christ known to all people.

(L to R) Rev. Don Heap, Leonard Desroches and Rev. Bob Holmes, October 4, 1998, in front of St. Paul's: "We come here today on the feastday of St. Francis of Assisi, who reminds us that renunciation of all war is the lasting foundation for genuine works of justice and mercy."

As it became clear that St. Paul's parish would not agree to our request, we met to pray and discern how to persist. We decided to extend the invitation far beyond the local parish—where the real responsibility lay. We realized that as a symbol of the Just War, this monument could be on the property of any of the other denominations. Our own press statement, which we read on the sidewalk in front of the memorial, on May 10, stated:

> The February 1998 threat of escalated war in Iraq spurred us to seek Christ's way to respond to war—to all war beyond this specific conflict.
>
> After weeks of prayer and discernment we feel bound in conscience to publicly witness to the urgent need for the church to begin concrete actions of *renunciation of the "Just War" doctrine*—beyond studies and statements. The Just War doctrine sanctions and therefore perpetuates war upon war, poverty here and abroad, an overwhelming, endless flood of refugees and irreparable damage to Earth.
>
> We fully respect the need for a memorial for the war dead and their loved ones. Our concern is only about one part of the memorial: *the sword at the centre of the cross*. This is for us a blasphemy—a total violation of the person and message of Christ. There could be no clearer symbol of the Just War doctrine which continues to be adhered to by the mainline churches—of which we are active members.
>
> Last week we came to pray and to offer leaflets to the members of the congregation here at St. Paul's. Today we come to extend our invitation far beyond this congregation. We come today to urge both St. Paul's parish and the representatives of all Toronto-area mainline churches to join together in this symbolic act of renunciation of war as a public witness to Christ's urgent, life-giving call to love our enemies.
>
> We offer mallet, chisel and crowbar to the representatives of St. Paul's and of the mainline churches…We urge them to see the urgency of action beyond studies and words.

Then we each read out loud our own individual statements:

> My name is Len Desroches...Last week, most members of St. Paul's congregation responded very well to our leafleting. But one member rushed by us saying sarcastically, "Maybe we should hang a swastika over the cross instead of the sword!" We are seriously lost as mainline churches. We do not know our own Christian history of radical nonviolent resistance to war, including resistance to Nazi militarism. All the states, except for Denmark, did not take seriously nonviolent resistance. As Catholic American monk Thomas Merton put it, "Denmark was not the only European nation that *disagreed* with Hitler...But it was one of the only nations which offered explicit, formal and successful nonviolent resistance to Nazi power." Since nonviolence was not seriously applied by most other governments, it is not possible to scientifically or logically claim that nonviolence could never have worked in the face of the Nazis. In fact, the one place where it was most intentionally applied—in Le Chambon, a village in Nazi-occupied France—nonviolence proved to be both dramatically effective and successful. Here, approximately 5,000 Christians risked their lives and hid approximately 5,000 Jews under the noses of the Nazis. In the end only two people lost their lives.
>
> It has been estimated by Harold M. Schulweis, rabbi of the Valley Beth Shalom in Encino California, that there were at least 50,000 mainly Christian rescuers of Jews all over Europe—with the possibility that 10 times that many took part in acts that involved risk. In other words: half a million Oskar Schindlers! (Schindler was a German Catholic industrialist. Some claim he saved more Jews from Nazi gas chambers at greater personal cost than any other single person during WWII. *Schindler's List*, the book and the movie, popularizes his story.)

> Hitler's chief propagandist declared: "Even if we lose [the war], we will win, because our ideals will have penetrated the hearts of our enemies." The ideal of the permanent war needs the ideal of the permanent war economy. Both ideals have penetrated our hearts. Every minute we continue to spend as a world community roughly $1,900,000 on the military while every minute 15 children die of hunger and inadequate health care. There is no way that the Nazis lost the moral war: the festering, pus-filled sores of day-to-day militarism cover this sweet earth like cancer from some massive, pathetic addiction.
>
> It is a lie that our only choice is to place either a sword or a swastika over the cross. Both the sword and the swastika represent the force of fear, hatred and killing. The plough and the cross represent the power of love; the plough and the cross represent both the soul force and the tools of nonviolence. We must choose as a church community. So I come with this hammer to offer to the representatives of all the mainline churches.

Next spoke Bob Holmes, a member of the Congregation of St. Basil (an order of Catholic priests), a former high school principal and a founder of the One World Global Education Program. At the time he was the director of seminarians for his order.

> Today I invite Cardinal Ambrozic, as the spiritual leader of the Catholic Archdiocese of Toronto, to join with the rector and wardens of St. Paul's Anglican Church, and leaders from all the mainline churches, in a symbolic action which will clearly demonstrate the renunciation of all war…
>
> I recall the witness of our patron St. Basil, who saw the new order under Constantine when the Church began giving its blessing to the army and to killing in the name of the state. Basil renounced the militarism of his day and named it murder.

> I offer this tool [crowbar] to Cardinal Ambrozic so that, in the name of all Roman Catholics, he may help remove the sword from the cross of Christ as the first step in transforming it into a symbol of peace—a plough—which, placed back on the cross, would remind all Christians of their call to be peacemakers not warriors.

Finally, Don, (Dan) Heap spoke. Don is a priest of the Anglican Church, and a member of the Holy Trinity Parish. He is a former member of both Toronto City Council and of the Canadian Parliament. Previous to that, after three years in charge of an Anglican parish, he spent 17 years as a factory labourer.

> Jesus Christ asks us to love our enemies and do good to those who hate us.
>
> Canadian church leaders ask governments to avoid *unnecessary* violence in war, especially against civilians, but to be ready to kill our enemies if we consider our war "just".
>
> Desmond Tutu, Anglican Archbishop of Cape Town, says: "We've got to get down to the business of training…people…in *nonviolent action and its spirituality*…being quite prepared to take the consequences of standing up on behalf of God's people."
>
> Why not take a sign of war, the sword, down from the cross, turn it into a ploughshare and put it back on the cross as a sign that we renounce war? I am here to offer this chisel to Bishop Finlay of the Anglican Diocese of Toronto for this work.

Hammer, chisel and crowbar

Our tools symbolized our decision to act beyond words and statements: vigils, fasts, leafleting and public commitment to risk arrest if at some point no church leader was willing to begin the process of taking down the sword from the cross.

We put our tools in front of us each time we met to pray and discern and organize as a reminder of the urgency of our task. We brought our tools to each public vigil to recall the very real tools of nonviolence.

CROSS AND PLOUGHSHARE OR CROSS AND SWORD? | 39

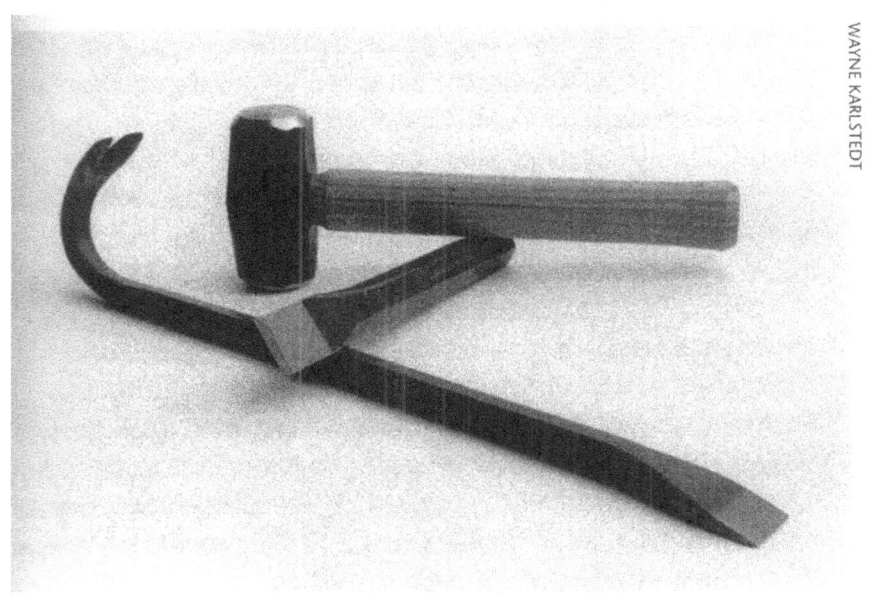

WAYNE KARLSTEDT

"And they shall hammer swords into ploughs." Isaiah 2:4
"We offer mallet, chisel and crowbar to the representatives of the mainline churches. We urge them to see the urgency of action beyond studies and words."
May 10, 1998 press statement.

(Top) Creative note-taking by Bob Holmes
(Above) Jim Loney of the Toronto Catholic Worker (left) in discussion with a passerby in front of St. Paul's Church during one of our vigils.

Half a year of prayer and action

In the heat of the summer of 1998, at a special retreat, the three of us came to terms with the fact that we were in this for a longer haul than we had anticipated. Confronting the state and corporations was one thing. Confronting and resisting our own faith community's complicity with warmaking, done in the spirit of honesty and respect, was much more demanding and was mainly uncharted territory.

Alice Heap (left) and William Payne (right) at one of our press conferences in front of St. Paul's with media and church security in the background.

We committed ourselves to offering a realistic time frame for the church leaders that would make a response possible. At the same time, we also committed ourselves to maintaining a sense of urgency. We therefore decided to organize *Half A Year of Monthly Prayer and Action* to open up a deeper space for the Holy Spirit to confront and heal us as a church. Each month, on a date representing Christian nonviolence, we would organize a public vigil in front of St. Paul's war memorial. Each vigil would be a public invitation and challenge for the church leaders to take down the sword. Finally, on April 2, 1999, Good Friday, we would invite the church leaders one last time, and if there was no response we would begin ourselves the process of removing the sword from the cross.

The first vigil took place on October 4, the feastday of Francis of Assisi. The others were on November 5, the date of the massacre at Damietta by the crusaders, which St. Francis witnessed and denounced; December 2, the assassination of Jean Donovan in El Salvador; January 15, feastday of Martin Luther King Jr.; February 22, the execution of Sophie and Hans Scholl, student leaders of the White Rose resistance movement in Nazi Germany; March 23, the eve of the assassination of Oscar Romero, recalling his cry "Cease the repression!"

We placed ads in the publications of the six mainline churches: Roman Catholic, Anglican, United, Presbyterian, Baptist and Lutheran. We then sent out press releases announcing our plan. To those assembled with us in front of St. Paul's war memorial on October 4, we declared,

> We come here today on the feastday of St. Francis of Assisi because he stands as one of the most dramatic examples of the saints and prophets of the church, who remind us that renunciation of all war is the lasting foundation for genuine works of justice and mercy...In a few minutes we hope to enter the fenced-off area here in front of the war memorial in order to offer hammer, chisel and crowbar to the church leaders for use in this urgent symbolic action. We call on the church authorities to break with its habit of turning to the state to protect the sword.

But the church did turn to the state. At the request of the church wardens, we were arrested for trespass. We were released shortly afterwards.

We had begun to call attention to the urgency of confronting the Sword at the heart of the church.

Our action began to raise questions and real feelings. Regina Silva Robinson wrote, in a letter to *The Anglican*: "As a member of St. Paul's, Bloor Street, I was both saddened and angered by what I saw on October 4 outside our church and later shown in the media...Yes, war is horrible. But those men and women fought and they fought for a reason--freedom...What better symbol of cutting through evil than a sword?"

Don and Hester Warne. Don, a Canadian war veteran, wrote to the author, "May the Spirit of God in this new millennium spur our mind to achieve a true reconciliation with our enemies."

K. Corey Keeble wrote in the same edition of *The Anglican*: "That these three iconoclasts have brazenly offered hammer, chisel and crowbar to do violence to the monument reveals the emptiness and hypocrisy of their supposed anti-war, anti-violence stance."

Charlie Angus, a regular columnist for *Catholic New Times*, wrote an impassioned and well-reasoned article questioning what we had done. "It doesn't matter whether a war memorial inspires awe, indifference or disgust in the eyes of the present generation," he wrote. Agreed. Our response came not from these emotions. It came from our conviction of conscience telling us (trial defendants and trial witnesses, including Bishop Gumbleton) that the sword on the cross is literally a blasphemy.

Charlie spoke of the "obligations of history." Agreed—if it includes the obligation to expose the lies of the history of war, especially the biggest lie of all: that our freedom comes from the destruction of millions of state-designated "enemies."

His article acknowledged our good intentions, noting that we "had hoped to implant a lesson about the dangers of militarism." Not exactly. Our action was a call to an absolute non-cooperation with the sin of militarism.

Finally, the article states: "I'd prefer to leave the coming generations with the freedom to decide for themselves. If the vets died for anything, at the very least, they died for that." One Canadian vet, Donald Warne of Whitby, Ontario, wrote me after the trial in support of our action:

> At age 19 I offered my life to my country as a volunteer in World War II. Because of my high school marks in math and science, I was trained as a radar technician. Eventually I was involved in the remote push button war of the 21st century. My team pushed that war to its extremes—the fire-bombing of men, women and children in Dresden, and the ultimate horror—the devastation of Hiroshima. That experience of dropping the atomic bomb on Hiroshima forever removed from my mind the concept that there could be a "just" war… May the Spirit of God in this new millennium spur our mind to achieve a true reconciliation with our enemies.

It was during our yearly Remembrance Day anti-war actions at Litton Systems in the 1980s that I learned that you cannot talk about "the vets" as a homogenous group: some vets publicly defended our actions against the objections of fellow vets. "There is nothing 'shabby' or 'shameful' about cruise missile protesters using Remembrance Day to call attention to our government's shabby and shameful decision to test the newest and most hideous nuclear weapon," wrote Legion member, Richard Lunn, in the *Toronto Star* on November 15, 1983.

Out of respect for all who disagreed with us, and especially for those who were hurt or angered by our actions, we took the time to answer all letters and to talk with people about their concerns. We had to accept that many would not agree with us.

We decided to send an occasional *Cross and Sword Newsletter* to our supporters—mostly to keep them informed, but also to ask for their help with certain tasks and various expenses, for example the cost of ads. In our first *Cross and Sword Newsletter*, December, 1998, we reflected:

> As a group, the three of us have faced hard questions and resolved some conflicts; we have also strengthened our resolve and our friendship; we continue an ongoing discipline of prayer, discernment and practical work.
>
> The hard work of tending to all aspects of an action is integral to genuine resistance. Serious resistance is not defined by the amount of prison time one serves, as one war resister wrongfully claimed. There are indeed times when God asks us to accept long jail sentences, but it is the spiritual quality of our lives that defines how "serious" our resistance is. It is entirely possible for an individual of a faith community to do resistance without facing its own conflicts; without being merciful; without really working towards reconciliation. This is serious resistance? The time and energy we give over to reconciliation among ourselves and with others is *not* "time taken away from the resistance." This does not delay the resistance, but puts it into God's timing.

The newsletter went on: "We are thankful for the straight-forward media coverage our witness has received." I was surprised at the amount of good media coverage over the course of the whole witness—from *Catholic New Times*, to the *Toronto Star*, to the CBC, to *The Anglican* and a number of other alternative sources such as the *ACTivist*, the *Christian Peacemaker Teams Newsletter* and the *Nuclear Resister (USA)*. This kind of issue so rarely gets serious treatment form the regular media. One article in the non-religious press went beyond just good coverage. Michael Valpy's piece in the *Globe and Mail*, Monday, May 29, 2000, was a rare, masterful presentation of the essence of the Cross and Sword witness.

Our newsletter continued:

> We've received phone calls, letters and e-mails of support, and some criticism and opposition. Don has received and responded to a letter from his bishop.

> Thanks very much to all of you who are praying with us, either present bodily at the war memorial, or wherever you must be.
>
> Thanks again to William Payne for his superb work on the two banners which frame all our actions.

I had put much prayer and discernment distilling into a few words the essence of our witness that could be contained by two banners. They would be crucial to making clear to the public why we were vigiling in front of the war memorial over the months. So it was important that they be well done. They were placed in very capable hands.

> Thanks to Andrew Cash who's put time and money into video recording [in order] to share our work of nonviolent resistance in the faith context with a greater number of people.
>
> Thanks to all of you who've helped to leaflet. A special thanks to those of you who've prepared and led the actual time of prayer on the site and to those of you who've agreed to do so for the coming vigils.
>
> If you feel called to join the civil disobedience part of the resistance, there are two important conditions: (1) that you be actively engaged in one of the mainline churches; (2) that you fully accept the decision that the risk of arrest is part of the Good Friday action; that we will actually aim to physically take the sword off the cross on Good Friday.
>
> Most of all, please join us for one hour of prayer each month! Your presence registers your own resistance to the church's continued adherence to the Just War doctrine. (It does not necessarily imply that you associate yourself with our willingness to commit civil disobedience.) Even more centrally, your presence makes clear your longing for the church community to come to terms with Christ's urgent call to learn to love our enemies. WARNING—because we are standing around, it's easy to get chilled now that the cold weather has started. Please remember to dress very warmly, especially for your feet.

At the December vigil in front of St. Paul's war memorial, Sister Mary Gauthier and Sister Mary Anne Olekszyk led us in a time of prayer in honour of the life and witness (martyrdom) of Jean Donovan, killed by the El Salvadoran military the same year that Oscar Romero was assassinated. We were moved by the unexpected presence of a young man from El Salvador, now living in Canada. He recounted how, as a boy, he was deeply affected by the murder of Jean and the other three women. *Presente!*

The January vigil was led by three Baptist friends, Ron Getz, Barb Getz and John David Ashworth. It was a rich celebration of the life and witness of Martin Luther King Jr. in the midst of large banks of fresh snow. I took my turn at the leafleting. It was gratifying to see how some people, who initially indicated that they weren't interested in taking a leaflet, changed their mind when I said: "Today is Martin Luther King's birthday."

We met twice with the group that plans the yearly ecumenical Good Friday walk. We went with no assumptions, exploring the most controversial issues as honestly as we could: civil disobedience and in particular, the act of physically taking off the sword. We listened to people's questions, concerns and fears. Out of a very fruitful exploration the following decisions were taken:

1. One of the 'stations of the cross' would focus on militarism. The three of us were asked to prepare and present this station.
2. Our Holy Week fast was in part to be an invitation for any and all who wished to spend some time exploring with us what it means to renounce all war and to learn, as mainline churches, to live out the implications of love and enemy.
3. Our action at the war memorial would take place **after** the Good Friday walk. Those who felt called to join us there were invited to do so.

There was not much snow at the February vigil, but it was very cold. Rob Schearer and Gabe Thirlwall from the *Student Christian Movement of the University of Toronto* (*SCM-UofT*) led us in prayer as we honoured the martyrdom of the students of the White Rose resistance to the Nazi government.

At the March vigil we meditated on the words of Oscar Romero: "The cause of all our problems is the oligarchy, that small nucleus of families who do not concern themselves with the plight of the people, except in so much as they have need of them as a source of cheap and plentiful labour…The armed forces are responsible for protecting the interests of the oligarchy…"

In our March, 1999 newsletter, the last one before Good Friday, we wrote:

> We urge you to consider what it means to live in a church whose claim to the right of mass killing and destruction ("war") undermines its works of charity, justice and mercy. What will we pass on to the young ones just beginning to explore whether they have a place in the church…Even if you are not completely resolved [about the nature of our action], nonetheless we urge you to set aside time, to come with friends and family (bring the children!) to help make our common yearning utterly clear: to be more fully a faith community… to move from renunciation to liberation…After centuries of terrible denial, it will take a strong, clear witness to begin to break open future possibilities of conversion—an miracles. The three of us have our own role, but this is a witness that belongs to all in the church community.

Risking faith
In prayer we challenged ourselves to be honest—to resist cynicism—about actually hoping for a miracle: some church leader(s) risking to publicly renounce the Just War teaching.

(Left to right) Don Heap, Len Desroches and Bob Holmes. Our banner's words distil the essence of our witness.

We committed ourselves to doing everything we could to facilitate such an event. We wrote individual letters to each one of the leaders of the six mainline churches, urging them to risk an urgently-needed act of faith.

Yet we also accepted that we needed to be prepared to be arrested on Good Friday if no one responded. A Holy Week fast was decided on. Two weeks prior to Holy Week, March 14 to 28, 1999, I began a three-week fast at my place, mainly as a way for Bob, Don and I to begin to set aside time to prepare for the Holy Week fast and the Good Friday action.

We wrote to the Toronto headquarters of the six mainline churches, letting them know that we would be present for an hour of prayer vigil outside each office at designated times on Monday and Tuesday of Holy Week and inviting them to join us then.

On Wednesday before Holy Wek, Anglican Bishop Finlay phoned to invite the three of us to meet him at his office, with two of his staff and the rector and wardens of St. Paul's, on Monday of Holy Week.

At the beginning of Holy Week, the three of us moved into a public space donated by a friend, Dave Walsh—the same sacred prayer space donated for the three-week 1991 Lenten fast against the Gulf War. Daily times of prayer were offered to the public: 8:00–8:30 a.m. and 7:30–8:30 p.m. Tuesday, March 30, there was a public evening to probe the implications of renouncing the Just War doctrine. On Monday and Tuesday, slightly weakened by the beginning of the fast, the three of us headed out to the churches' headquarters as planned—except the Anglican Church one, since we would be meeting with Bishop Finlay. We were met by someone at each of the other stops—except at the Catholic Archdiocesan Centre. We had good conversations with the office of Presbyterians, Baptists and Lutherans. Since the United Church representatives were in Ottawa, we visited with Janet Somerville, the Executive Secretary of the Canadian Council of Churches, located in the same building. She then invited us to pray with her in the chapel.

The meeting in Bishop Finlay's office was very encouraging. The bishop was not afraid of allowing an atmosphere of direct speaking and questioning by all. Though neither we nor the other six changed our positions, we came to a better understanding of each other. As Don put it: "Thank God that Bishop Finlay continues to be a very good pastor." The bishop's response to the issue, and especially his capacity to challenge and yet respect Don as one of the priests in his charge, are all signs of hope for the church community. It inspired a letter to *The Anglican* by Anna Jarvis, which gives words to what many Christians feel today:

> I want to commend Bishop Finlay for his response to the sword and cross action…I was surprised and excited to hear that the bishop had stepped in to help mediate between the three involved in the action and St. Paul's. It was a courageous step.
>
> As a disaffected Anglican, I have been encouraged by his action to reconsider the relevance the church has in my life. Twenty years ago I rejected the church as an institution, in part because I found nothing in it that gave meaning to my work around social justice and nonviolence. Yes, there

were works of charity in my church, but no deep analysis or activities to suggest that the Anglican faith was examining itself as well as working to eradicate the deeper roots of poverty, inequality and injustice.

Some years ago I became aware that there was a radical Christian community, here in Toronto and around the world, that actually saw faith as the foundation of its work for social justice and nonviolence...

Although I am a historian by education and an Anglican by upbringing, I did not know that the early church was against war, as the Mennonites and Quakers are today. I sense that the current slump the Anglican Church is now facing (my childhood church in Ottawa recently sold some of its property, on which town houses are now built) could change, were it to return to these radical roots. The church would gain a relevance and a dynamism that would certainly draw in young and not-so-young people like me.

As a historian, it saddens but does not surprise me that the history of nonviolence is invisible. Our ignorance of this history and the lessons it carries allows us to claim that war and violence are the only way to resolve conflict. Our ignorance of our own church's history and our denial of the radical meaning of Christ's own words allow us to claim that our own scriptures sanction war...

With our country presently in a state of war, the church must keep asking itself whether its own gospel calls it to support state-sanctioned war or to the far greater challenge of nonviolence and love of enemy.

Good Friday, 1999

On Good Friday we were surprised when Stuart Coles, one of the organizers of the yearly ecumenical walk, opened the event with a very prayerful public reading of my full-page manifesto on love of enemy and freedom which had appeared in *Catholic New Times*:

> Is my enemy the one who prevents my "freedom" or is my enemy the one who exposes my deep lack of inner freedom— my debilitating lack of faith in the real power of Love and consequently my damaging lack of self-love and courage?

Personally, I encounter enemies all the time: those who touch parts of my broken self. I could easily start a war almost every day. (Many people *do* live in perpetual warfare, hot, cool or cold. Do they experience more freedom?)

My enemy is the one who confronts me with daily choices. Will I transform my fear and anger into a force for hatred and violence or a force for love? Is security measured by my possessions? Is freedom gained by paying for mass killing through taxes and for destruction through war? Or are security and freedom deeper spiritual realities which can only be maintained by spiritual power?…

I know to whom I owe my freedom: to the countless women and men, known and unknown, who have refused to hate and kill, who today refuse to hate and kill; who resist greed in themselves and in institutions, knowing that we can never be free as long as we are willing to kill for wealth; who practise mercy as well as justice; and most of all, who refuse to stop loving.

I owe my freedom:

* to the early church community who refused to participate in the state's warfare;
* to Francis and Clare of Assisi;
* to Fray Antonio de Montesinos who risked his life denouncing his fellow Spaniards' gold-driven violence towards the indigenous people of Hispaniola;

I owe my freedom to the parishioners of Le Chambon who risked their lives and meagre possessions resisting Nazism and hiding Jewish children;

* to Hans Scholl of the White Rose student resistance movement in the heart of Nazi Germany, who cried out on his way to execution: "Long live freedom!"

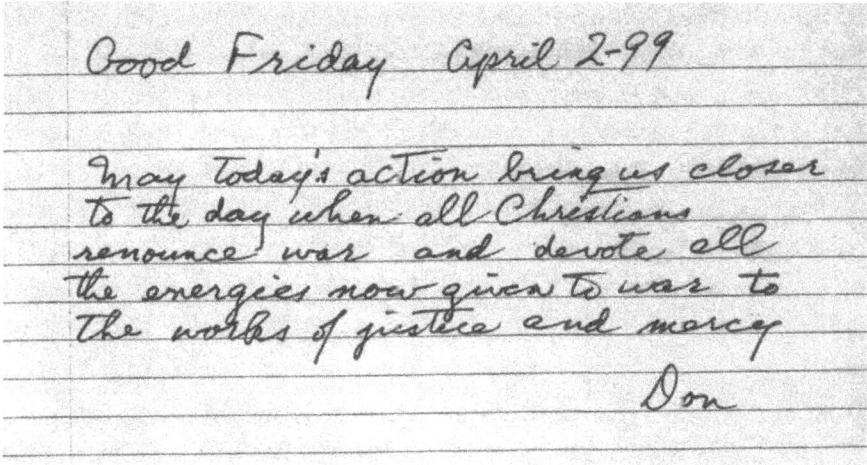

April 1999 Lenten Fast Journal

* to Jesuit priest Max Josef Metzer who, while awaiting execution by the Nazis wrote, "We need to organize for peace the way that men have organized for war."
* to Bishop Kiril of Bulgaria and his parishioners, who were prepared to lay their bodies on the railway track to protect Jews from the Nazi army (90 percent of Bulgarian Jews were saved);
* to Aristides de Sousa Mendes, who disobeyed orders as Portuguese consul general in Bordeaux, France, saving the lives of 10,000 Jews by illegally stamping passports. (His government stripped him and his family of job and benefits, but he said, "I accept everything that has befallen me with love.")
* to Franz Yagerstatter, an Austrian farmer executed by the Nazis for refusing to join the army, who wrote to his wife from prison: "God gives…a strength far stronger than all the might of the world."

> I owe my freedom to Rosa Parks, Martin Luther King, Jean Donovan, Thomas Merton, J.S. Woodsworth and Dorothy Day.
> To these, and to countless others, I owe the freedom that no enemy can ever take from me, the freedom that is not dependent on endless war and the perpetual war economy.

More recently, I owe my freedom to the members of "Las Abejas" (The Bees), an indigenous ecumenical pacifist group in Chiapas, Mexico, working for social justice but refusing to take up arms. On December 22, 1997, paramilitary groups entered the small village of Acteal and massacred 45 of their members, mostly women and children, as they fasted and prayed for an end to the violence in Chiapas. Women survivors have made it clear that their dead "live through us every day and sustain us."

Right after calling us to love our enemies, Christ calls us to be as "mature" in love as God is. Most of our translations use the word "perfect" rather than "mature." But as farmer and scripture scholar Clarence Jordan pointed out, the original word Jesus used had more to do with maturing, as a fruit grows into maturity: "To talk about unlimited retaliation is babyish; to speak of limited retaliation is childish; to advocate limited love is adolescent; to practice unlimited love is evidence of maturity." To become mature, to become free, is to renounce violence—and the fear and greed that drive it.

Our clinging, officially or unofficially, to the false doctrine of the "just war"—our fearful refusal to officially and publicly renounce it—undermines all our works of charity, justice and mercy. We remain childish or adolescent in our collective love. In the face of the daily brutality and impoverishment inflicted by the institution of war—the (only!) institution we pay to "deal" with our designated enemies—what power does the church's voice have? I personally do not know anyone who is deeply challenged or inspired by the pronouncements of such a compromised church which has barely begun to live out the radical, life-giving love of enemy.

May the Spirit, through the love of enemy, guide us as a church community to a more mature love. May She guide us to fuller freedom.

After the walk, a group of about 100 supporters joined us in front of St. Paul's war memorial. There, in their presence and in the presence of thirty riot police and some media, the three of us read aloud our press statement:

Through half a year of monthly vigils, articles, letters to the editors, radio and television interviews, and a Holy Week fast we have repeated our invitation…We offer mallet, chisel and crowbar for use in this symbolic action. We will pray and wait briefly one last time in the hope that some church leader will lead us in this witness. If nothing happens, the three of us feel bound in conscience to begin this task ourselves.

Finally, it is extremely important to point out that in one way or another all the churches, through St. Paul's Anglican, will in a few minutes be making one of the following critical decisions: they will lead us in taking down the sword from the cross; or they will allow the three of us to take down the sword from the cross—in both cases signalling their willingness to begin to renounce the just war doctrine; or they will do what they have done since the year 313, when Emperor Constantine declared Christianity the official, state-protected religion of the empire and its military: the church will choose to protect the sword with the physical force of the state; it will refuse to remove the sword from the cross; it will refuse to renounce the mass killing and destruction of the institution of war.

Good Friday is the one sacred day of the year when we come together as a church community and face once again the meaning of the Cross. Is the Cross a mere version of the Sword (as it has been and continues to be experienced by so many people), or is the Cross the sacred symbol of the fullness of love—including love of enemy? How we as a church community answer that question affects the whole human family.

Please join us in silent prayer.

After this silent prayer, when it became clear that no church leader would step forward, the three of us started to climb the fence surrounding the war memorial to begin to take the sword off the cross. Tim Corlis, a friend who once attended St. Paul's and who is now in the process of exploring membership in the Mennonite Church, noticed that one of the police officers looked emotionally stirred and upset. The officer stopped his activities and went behind a van. Another officer took his place

We were arrested and taken away in a police van. We spent a few hours at a local police station being questioned, finger-printed and booked on the criminal charge of *Mischief Over $5,000*, carrying a maximum possible jail sentence of either 10 years or 6 months, depending on how the crown elected to proceed. We were given a court date and finally released.

It was only after repeated court appearances—seven of them—that we were able to set a trial date: May 15, 2000.

Because the trial was almost a year away, we made a major commitment to organize a three-week public pre-trial fast and a very special evening on the eve of the trial, Sunday, May 14, 2000.

In the meantime we organized a "First Pre-Trial Event—An Evening of Listening and Advice—December 7, 1999 at Friends House." Early in our preparations for the trial we wanted to spend an evening with our supporters, listening carefully to their suggestions, questions and advice. We wrote in our December 1999 newsletter: "Some of you receiving this newsletter will not be in agreement with us, but are eager for a church as faithful to Jesus as possible. We intend to listen and to hear as honestly as possible."

War and Poverty—a Public Fast

We began to prepare for a three-week pre-trial Lenten fast: Monday April 3 to Good Friday April 21, 2000. Its focus was to be *"Renunciation of the Perpetual War Economy and its Resulting Poverty."*

The fast took place at Trinity-St. Paul's United Church. Anyone was welcome to drop in anytime between 7:30 a.m. and 9:30 p.m. for silence and meditation. Times of communal prayer were 7:30 a.m. and 7:30 p.m. Each Tuesday evening for the three weeks we offered a discussion related to war, poverty and love of enemy.

My first entry in the fast journal notes:

> Outside, a grey, damp day. Inside, in a basement room at Trinity-St. Paul's United Church ("The Rainbow Room") our fast begins.
>
> A few chairs, cushions and candles. Luckily, a window. Water and juice. Our ever-present tools (hammer, chisel and crowbar) to remind us of the urgency to go beyond studies and statements—to move concretely in turning sword to plough.

> Trinity-St. Paul's has been welcoming and supportive—not only offering this space but gathering some volunteers to greet people who might join us for morning prayer.
>
> Last night Don and I began our fast by sleeping at Friends House (Quakers) a few blocks from here. Bob Holmes will join us there during Holy Week. (In the meantime he will join us during the day on as regular basis as his schedule allows.)
>
> Always, the beginning of a fast like this is a challenge to be centred in a real faith in what we are living through—a radically different pace; a space (physical and spiritual) without unnecessary props; a sacred time to deepen faith and hope. Vulnerability. Faith in the very real power of love to transform sword into plough. Faith in the essential goodness of each other. Faith in the very real relationship with the One who first loved us.
>
> On the walls of our fast site there are children's 'primitive' attempts to name life's mysteries (this room is the Sunday School space). I look at the drawings of little humans beginning to name radical things like respect, cooperation, Christ, love,…Seems appropriate to our reasons for being here: fasting as a cry for life—and life in abundance.

A few days later I pointed out to Don a sign outside our room: "Juniors, grade 1–3." I joked: "I think that's in reference to our spiritual level." Don smiled. He seemed to agree.

A few of my other entries describe the usual ebb and flow of public fasts:

> Saturday morning, April 8—A very quiet Saturday morning. Don and I were by ourselves for prayer. (The other day I was the only one here for prayer.) A very good reminder of how a fast is more 'vertical' than 'horizontal'—if that's a helpful image. That is, a fast is not a rally or demonstration, where the sheer number of people is important (horizontal) and where there isn't a lot of one-to-one (vertical) time to be present to one another.

A public, open fast has its own unpredictable rhythm: lots of people come by when you don't expect; no one comes by when you were sure people were coming.

This Las Abejas family received 70 refugees into their two-room house following the massacre in the village of Acteal in the state of Chiapas, Mexico.

Wed. Apr 12, '00—I had anticipated that this public fast would be busy. It's even busier than anticipated—ongoing details here (maintaining the site, phone calls, clear communication with the church here,...) and the ongoing work for the trial and the eve before.

People come from various situations—some come with their precious vulnerability: violent co-worker; the pain of searching and waiting for work;...

All of a sudden I smell the stunning scent of delicious food from somewhere down the hall. Always, always, in a fast, I experience the *sheer beauty of food!* And the sheer beauty of taking time to share food with other(s).

Went for a short walk in the sun—basking in the free vitamin D.

Palm Sunday, April 16—A man who lives on the streets and sleeps in Out-of-the-Cold churches dropped in for a visit. His name is Ken. He's on a disability pension—which has been temporarily suspended. He has two sons who work and go to school. He came to chat and warm up a bit.

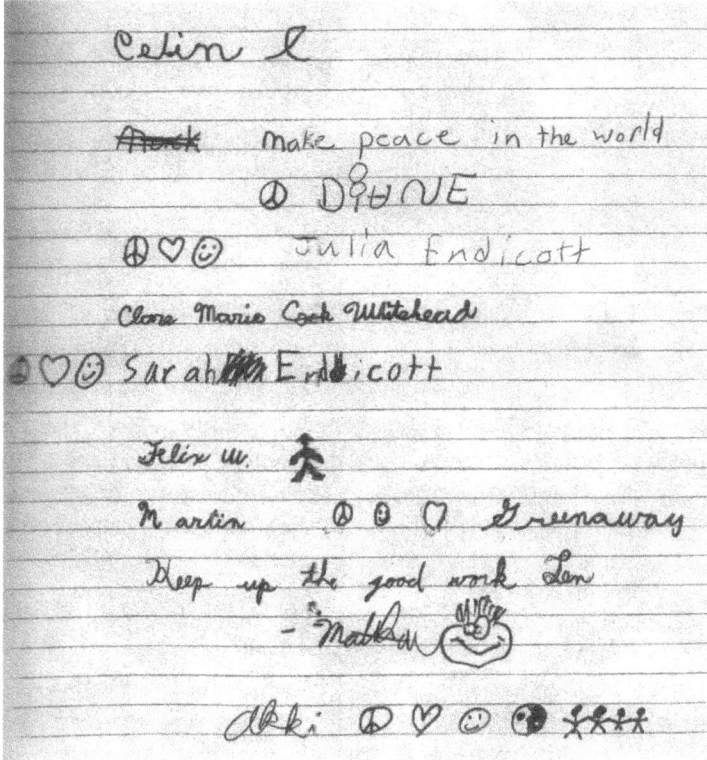

Fast journal entre by Trinity Saint-Paul's Sunday School, grades four to six.

This morning I preached the homily at St. Stephen-in-the-Fields—the church which is hosting our pre-trial evening. A wonderful, small congregation—good mixture of ages and races.

Then Don and I participated in a discussion about the issues of the fast with a social injustice committee here at Trinity-St. Paul's.

> A good ebb and flow of visitors.
> Tomorrow Hobo [Bob Holmes] joins us for Holy Week.
> Evening prayer in a few minutes.
> The yellow tulips have started to open up.
>
> April 19, 2000—From our fast site in the basement of the church, I step outside into the back yard: buds and grass and flowers—that tireless miracle of Spring!
>
> When I woke up and came to our fast site I'd forgotten it was my birthday. Anna [Jarvis] joined us and surprised me with a gift of organic juice. Good place to spend a birthday—praying and fasting and discussing with friends.
>
> The black and white cate granted us another visit this morning. (He even left a 'gift' behind once.)

Don's entry on the same date expresses the sentiments of all of us who shared our lives with each other in the Rainbow Room: "This fast is good. The sharing between Len, Bob and me, especially leading up to the Sunday 14 meeting and Monday trial, but also just in friendship…I look forward to the end of our fast with mixed feelings."

One of the most demanding dimensions of the pre-trial evening was organizing the participation in our trial by members of the "Las Abejas," the Christian, ecumenical, indigenous group committed to nonviolence in Chiapas, Mexico. We had just received news that two members had agreed to be "witnesses" at our trial: Antonio Gutierrez Perez and Maria Perez Vasquez, a married couple. Our friend Diego Mendez agreed to be our envoy: to go to Chiapas to meet with them and to accompany them here.

There were four other people who agreed to be witnesses at our trial:

- Bishop Thomas Gumbleton (RC) of Detroit has taken the risks and paid the price for his decades of faithfulness to active gospel nonviolence. He is also pastor of a poor, mainly black inner city parish in Detroit.
- Rev. Jeannie Loughrey is the priest at All Saints Anglican Church Community Centre in downtown Toronto. All Saints has worked for decades with those marginalized from society, including the homeless. As a pastor close to the victims of economic violence,

Jeannie knows the connections between the perpetual war economy and poverty.
- Cathy Crowe is a nurse and advocate for the homeless. She works with the Toronto Disaster Relief Committee which advocates for the "1% Solution" for affordable housing as a real part of the solution for homelessness. Cathy has resisted Canadian militarism. She understands that militarism and homelessness are not two separate issues.
- Janet Somerville is the General Secretary of the Canadian Council of Churches and former editor of *Catholic New Times*. She has a deep passion for the spiritual health of the whole church community and its need to come to terms with its role in warfare.

Since this was a trial dealing with the church and war and there were already many church people as witnesses, it was agreed, on Cathy's suggestion, that she would not be called upon unless necessary.

At some point, we found out that Janet had been invited to be part of a delegation to Iraq on behalf of the Canadian Council of Churches. During the fast, she dropped off her statement which we planned to read to the judge in her absence. In the end the statement was never read, because the trip to Iraq was cancelled and Janet was able to be present at our trial. Nonetheless some of her insights in that first written statement are worth noting here:

> The debate about Christian discipleship and war is almost as old as the church. For people who want to accept the Gospel but also want to be "realistic" and responsible citizens of the world, it is a very heavy question. Biblical texts can be made to weigh in on either side of the debate. Indeed, for a Christian wrestling with this question, it is not so much what Jesus said as what Jesus did...Jesus chose to go undefended to the cross. The Roman Empire, inventor of the political crucifixion, was a master of the uses of war, as all successful empires have been. The encounter between Jesus and the Roman empire did not result in a negotiated compromise. It resulted in Jesus' death by official public torture: a death, I believe, says something terrible about the spiritual character of any empire. A fervent guerilla war against the Roman empire was already afoot in

Jesus' own day. Jesus radically resisted the reign on Rome, but he did not join those who were resisting it with violent methods. The more deeply people ponder Jesus' rejection of empire and his even clearer rejection of the rule of money, the more likely they are to appreciate the reason why nonviolence is a form of Christian discipleship…

An intellectually honest use of the just war doctrine can result in a great deal of conscientious objection to actual wars. For example, the present Archbishop Primate of the Anglican Church of Canada recently cited the traditional just war doctrine when he refused to approve of Canada's participation in NATO's war-like action in Serbia and Kosovo.

Other Canadian Christian denominations who disapproved NATO's resort to war in the Serbia-Kosovo case did not use the language of the just war doctrine to do so. It is my impression that they deliberately avoided that language because there is increasing unease among Christian thinkers about the concept of a "just war". Many consider that modern weaponry, with its high-tech destructiveness, has rendered impossible a war that is "just" by the traditional standards. That is part of what Pope Paul VI meant in his famous speech before the United Nations when he called for war to be confined "to the museum of history", crying out: "No more war! War never again!" It is part of what the World Council of Churches means by inviting all its member churches to begin soon a "Decade Against Violence" that it hopes will educate the Christian imagination in the direction of systematic, thoughtful and prayerful nonviolence…

…there have always been Christian pacifists (at least, for as long as there have been Christians), convinced that to live the Gospel of Jesus Christ is radically incompatible with warmaking. Pacifists have, however, been in the minority among Christian believers. Since the Second World War, the overall intellectual movement in the churches has been away from the legitimation of war. Respect for rejection of all war, on the basis of Christian conviction, has been growing within the churches.

> No wonder, then, that the three Christian pacifists appearing in this court today have concluded that now might be a God-chosen time to challenge the church as a whole to renounce war…
>
> Now why would the three choose as a symbol an action which, on the face of it, is illegal?…
>
> God's law must outweigh human law for people who believe that there is a divine revelation which can be grasped by a faithful conscience…People who would never under any circumstances break a human law lack something in their appreciation of what it is to serve a living God whose will it is to convert human beings and transform human society. On the other hand: people who casually or selfishly defy civil authority lack something in their appreciation of how human societies achieve a measure of peace…
>
> Looking at it from a church perspective, it would be very strange to find them "guilty". It would not be strange to find them radical and disturbing. What they disturb, however, is not the peace imparted to the first Christian disciples by the risen Jesus. What they disturb is a placidity that sets into the souls of Christians who, like me and like most of us, are too fully at home in the world as it is, and who stop short of following the leading of God's revelation all the way to its awesome, unpredictable consequences.

During the fast we met with our lawyer Peter Rosenthal. Peter takes on only cases arising from resistance to militarism and injustice. He has worked with a number of us in the past. He is one of those rare lawyers who puts himself at the service of the issue at hand, as opposed to controlling the process for his own agenda. I first started working with Peter during my years resisting the building of the Cruise Missile at Litton Systems. A more recent and precedent-setting trial in which Peter was involved related to a resistance action in support of the Innu's resistance to NATO's low-level military war practice.

As usual, working with Peter is a transparent process where we identify our goals and he offers legal frameworks that could facilitate the task. We made clear that the most important thing in this trial was to put before the court the central issues of love of enemy and renunciation of the Just War teaching. We also decided, before the trial, that the three of us had made our contribution in relationship to the particular monument at St. Paul's. We made a clear decision that we were not going back to the monument at this time, even if we were not imprisoned. In fact, we believed that to pursue the physical removal of the sword from the cross would—at least at this time—distract from the real issue: the public, official renunciation of the Just War teaching. This does not mean that others might not be called in the future to pursue the task.

Like all public fasts, there were also quiet but sacred moments of gratitude, hope, and mutual encouragement. Yvonne from the Toronto Catholic Worker joined us and enriched the focus of the fast, knitting it into her work with the "so-called mentally ill." From a one-year-old's scribble, to a poet's offering, to an unexpected joke, to an elder's eloquent words, our fast journal was filled with rich reflections. This public fast journal—along with others over the years—remains a lasting testament to the precious faith insights of such times set aside to refuse to be falsely consoled while refusing to give in to despair.

"Is war ever just? Three priests respond
Besides the special pre-trial evening, the afternoon of May 14 was also set aside for a rare forum on the question, *Is War Ever Just?* It was organized by one of our trial witnesses, Rev. Jeannie Loughrey. Bishop Finlay introduced and moderated the meeting of nearly forty people. As Don noted: "It is rare—if not unprecedented—that a Canadian diocesan bishop give such recognition to that question."

Rev. Eric Beresford, ethicist co-ordinator for the Anglican Church of Canada, gave the meeting an outline of the question's history. Major (the Reverend) Eric T. Reynolds, Anglican Chaplain to the Armed Forces, gave the argument for the "Just War" teaching. He spoke of pacifism as being good, but emphasized that at times nations may need to "resort to force." Like most Christians, his greatest misunderstanding of gospel nonviolence was in failing to recognize it as a force—as the literal force of love—with its own powerful tools. His paper was entitled: "Is the Use of Force Morally Justifiable in the Protection of Values?" Force is not only justifiable in the protection of values, it is a moral obligation to use force. For me the authentic faith question is: "*Which* Force is Morally Justifiable in the Protection of Values?"

One of Major Reynolds' declarations perfectly mirrors the sword attached to the cross: "As a priest, I have my feet firmly planted in the 'City of God'…I preach the Gospel of peace, love and respect for the dignity of every human being. On the other hand, as a member of the human family, and as someone who has served and continues to serve Queen, country and the members of the Canadian Forces as a military chaplain, I recognize that my feet are also planted in the 'City of Man.'" Both the Cross and the Sword. As the francophone version of 'O Canada' has it: '…ton bras sait porter l'épée; it sait porter la croix.' ('…your arm knows how to carry the sword; it knows how to carry the cross.')"

Bob (Holmes) was the third person on the panel. He asked:

> Can we see Jesus with a gun? Dropping napalm? Dropping bombs?…Second only to love of God, who is love itself, is the commandment to love our neighbour and, as we learn in the parable of the Good Samaritan, this includes even those we distinguish as foreign and inimical to us…Christians have justified wars and crusades and pogroms and missile strikes and nuclear weapons and Trident submarines…we don't really learn well from the past…A "peace" gained by violence can only be maintained by the threat of more violence. It may be the "Pax Romana" or the "Pax Americana" but it is not the "Shalom" which Jesus promised…the world has been militarized to an extent far greater than Hitler ever envisioned, where oceans are patrolled by Trident submarines and the skies can be filled with SAC bombers—all in the name of "Peace" which is *not* peace but is, in reality, the protection of the wealthy from the poor, through the imposition of the economics of global greed backed up by the military might of the New Empire—the USA and NATO allies (including Canada)…Jesus, in teaching us to love our enemy, does not tell us to be submissive, [but calls us] to non-violent resistance and non-cooperation with evil. Jesus confronted the religious and political oppression of his day and accepted the consequences—arrest, trial, torture and execution—trusting in a God who calls us to love our enemies and even forgiving his executioners as he died. The cross and resurrection are

God's answer to the violence of oppression…War is never the way!

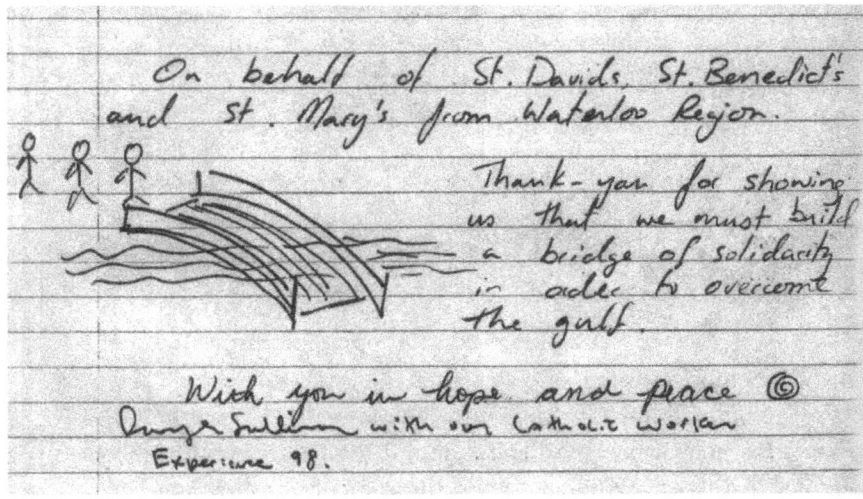

Fast journal entry by Dwyer Sullivan

Nations Shall Learn War No More
The special pre-trial evening liturgy was held at the Anglican Church of St. Stephen-in-the-Fields where Kevin Flynn is the priest. It was ably facilitated by Mary Gauthier and Loraine Land. The church was packed, overflowing to the gallery. The beating heart of the entire evening was *love of enemy and renunciation of the "just war."* Silence was woven into music by Robbie Beaumont, songs by Joanne Clark and liturgical dance by Karusia Wroblewski Flynn.

Each of our trial witnesses shared some reflections with us—making the connections between relentless militarism and relentless poverty: Bishop Thomas Gumbleton, Janet Somerville, Reverend Jeannie Loughrey and Cathy Crowe. The only witnesses who couldn't be there in person were the representatives of *Las Abejas*, a pacifist, indigenous Christian group in Chiapas, Mexico. One of their members had been killed a few days prior.

It was Mothers' Day—founded as a day to resist war—and so we asked two mothers, Sheila Sullivan and Joanne Clark, to read messages from friends in the resisting church: Phil Berrigan in prison; Hildegard

Goss-Mayr of the International Fellowship of Reconciliation; members of The Lantern, a Christian Life Centre in Newfoundland and the Canadian Religious Conference. (Their words are heard in the next chapter.)

Alice Heap and helpers led us in a break during which time the hat was passed around. Thanks to the real commitment of the assembly, along with the donations that had been previously sent, enough money was raised to cover the costs of honoraria, travel and the purchase of the trial transcript.

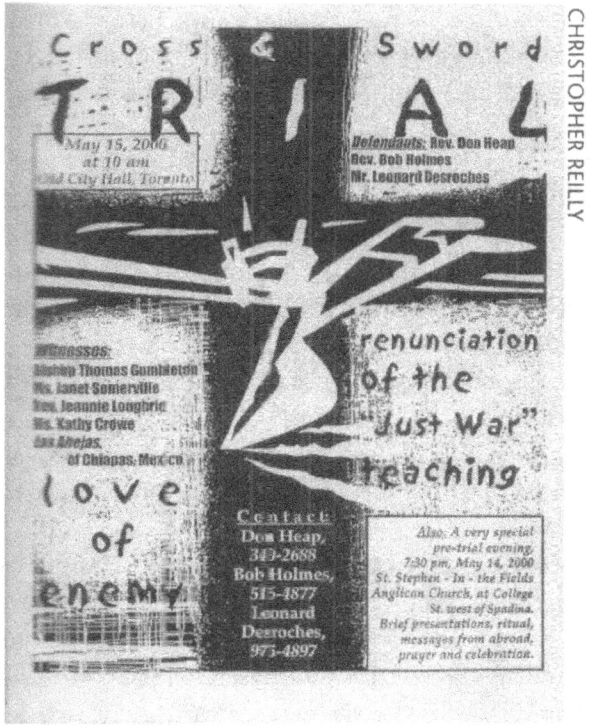

Poster announcing the Cross and Sword Trial.

In the absence of Las Abejas, the indigenous group from Chiapas, we prayed out loud the names of their martyrs at Acteal in 1997, as well as the names of those who had died of homelessness on our Toronto streets:

- *Streets of Toronto*: Brent Simms; Tom French; Jeff Holyhome; Eugene Upper; Irwin Anderson; Mirsalah-Aldin Kompani;

Edmond Wai Hong Yu; Richard Roy; Wally Neshkiwe; Linda Houston; Douglas Currie; Marie Louise Sharrow; David Solomon; Andre Choquette; Bill Carson; Dwight Solomon; Ron Pearce; Garland Shepherd; Patrick Pangowish; Stanley Peterson; Calvin Waindubence; Michael Fairthorne; Jimmy Reuben; John Kovacs; Julius Krsinksy; Lester Pawis; John Austin; Adam Soltysik; Vernon Crow; Kathleen Hart.

- *Las Abejas martyrs:* Marcela Capote Ruiz; Miguel Jimenez Perez; Lorenzo Gomez Perez; Regina Luna Perez; Marcela Vasquez Vasquez; Rosa Perez Perez; Micaela Pukuj Luna; Ignacio Pukuj Luna; Antonia Vasquez Vasquez; Pablina Hernandez Vasquez; Veronica Vasquez Luna; Veronica Perez Oyalte; Juana Luna Vasquez; Juana Perez Perez; Juana Vasquez Perez; Alejandro Luna Ruiz; Augustin Gomez Ruiz; Maria Luna Mendez; Rosa Vasquez Luna; Micaela Vasquez Luna; Rosa Gomez Perez; Maria Ruiz Oyalte; 3 unnamed; Catalina Luna Ruiz; Rosalina Luna Perez; Daniel Gomez Perez; Jaime Luna Ruiz; Graciela Gomez Hernandez; Rosela Gomez Hernandez; Manuela Paciencia Moreno; Victorio Vazquez Perez; Josefa Vasquez Perez; Juan Carlos Luna Perez; Augustin Ruiz Gomez; Catalina Vazquez Perez; Alonso Vasquez Gomez; Sebastian Gomez Perez; Juana Vasquez Luna; Marcela Capote Vasquez; Guadalupe Gomez Hernandez.

In the tradition of honouring those who have died and are present in faith, we prayed the Spanish response *"PRESENTE!"* after each name. It was a powerful meditation on life, death and resurrection.

The defendants (Don, Bob and myself) led a closing ritual wherein a member from each of the six mainline churches made a symbolic commitment to "continuing the work in our own church communities." Each of the six—Anne Mutch, Anglican; John David Ashworth, Baptist; Sheila Sullivan, Roman Catholic; Jim Kirkwood, United Church; Charlotte Stuart, Presbyterian; Troy Beretta, Lutheran—was given a hammer and a garden tool. The hammer represented the active nonviolent resistance (the "NO!"), and the garden tool represented the planting of alternatives (the "YES!"). *LOVE YOUR ENEMIES* was carved on the handle of each tool.

The evening ended with enthusiastic singing and dancing to the round that had gathered us at the beginning of the evening:

And everyone 'neath their vine and fig tree,
shall live in peace and not afraid;
and into ploughshares bend their swords,
nations shall learn war no more.

3 A Cloud of witnesses

The trial

An introduction
As part of the consequences of an honest nonviolent civil disobedience action, it seems to me important to accept the possibility that very few people—or maybe no one—will show up at your trial You must still speak the truth with full dignity. At the same time you do all you can to make sure people do know that they are needed, that they are full participants with you and are deeply welcomed. Radical hospitality extends even into the courtroom designed to intimidate.

We did not know how many people would come to our trial, but I felt it important to be prepared in case a large number did show up. So I persisted in requesting the largest possible courtroom. On the day of the trial, Monday May 15, 2000, the largest courtroom in Toronto's Old City Hall Courthouse was packed—with persistent elders, curious high school students, one dedicated reporter, involved church people, faithful friends and family members.

The large and lively turnout seemed a very fitting way to honour the sacred task at hand: coming together as a church community and friends in a room provided by the state to confront the feared mystery of love of enemy; to name out loud the urgent consequent task of renouncing the "Just War" teaching; to enter more fully into this conversation which we so often pass over in our churches. Even the use of three experienced lawyers, which at first struck me as extravagant, became a visible statement to the justice system that it too was going to have to stretch beyond the narrow confines of law and order into the realm of not only justice, but also of mercy.

As we entered the courthouse we were searched and then directed down the corridors lined with the accused of society. The gathering of a vibrant community of faith in the halls of the "justice system" was a sign of hope. For me, this whole witness and action had been an attempt to plant a seed more deeply—much more deeply. Dorothy Ross, one of Canada's war veterans, commented after the trial: "The most important lesson for me was how the small seed grew. I had known about these intentions to draw attention to the monument at St. Paul's earlier and recognized some of the hostility you would all face. I had decided not to participate, feeling in my heart it was all useless. And I was overwhelmed by the Gulf War. The end result of the courageous witness had been a courtroom overflowing with people—most of them young. Throughout the day I could *hear* the silence. It was a profoundly dramatic day that moved me to a new depth of understanding of the spiritual strength of nonviolence."

That was May 2000. Now something extraordinary has happened!

The courtroom has been greatly enlarged in order to make room for a magnificent cloud of witnesses: judges and bishops arrested for resisting militarism; monks denouncing the brutality of greed; experienced politicians calling for a whole new political foundation based on the power of active nonviolence; former military men exposing the spiritual sickness of war; archbishops ordering soldiers to obey God and lay down their arms; biblical scholars exposing the myth of "redemptive violence"; labour leaders discovering nonviolence as much more than just a tactic; parents learning to resist; poets using pen to cut open the infection… all these and many more have joined us! Together in one courtroom, their collective voice is a stunning witness to this force of love we call "nonviolence." Though their voices have resounded for centuries, too many people still have not even heard, let alone deeply listened.

Never have they come together like this in one courtroom. Until now.

The courtroom doors are left open. A few spokespersons for the Institution of War have also come in. They have been allowed to have their say. Let each one be heard. Let the truth speak for itself. Let the truth set us free.

In this fuller forum, let the trial begin!

THE WITNESSES

THE ONTARIO COURT OF JUSTICE

HER MAJESTY THE QUEEN
v.
ROBERT HOLMES, LEONARD DESROCHES, DANIEL HEAP

PROCEEDINGS AT TRIAL

BEFORE THE HONOURABLE MR. JUSTICE C. PARIS
On May 15, 2000, at Toronto, Ontario.

CHARGE: Mischief Over

> IT IS VERY EASY TO BE SERVANTS OF THE WORD WITHOUT DISTURBING THE WORLD: A VERY SPIRITUALIZED WORD, A WORD WITHOUT ANY COMMITMENT TO HISTORY, A WORD THAT CAN SOUND IN ANY PART OF THE WORLD BECAUSE IT BELONGS IN NO PART OF THE WORLD. A WORD THAT CREATES NO PROBLEMS, STARTS NO CONFLICTS.
> **Archbishop Oscar Romero**

APPEARANCES:

Counsel for the Crown	E. Carrington, Esq.
Counsel for the Accused R. Holmes	S. Salvaterra, Esq.
Counsel for the Accused L. Desroches	P. McComb, Esq.
Counsel for the Accused D. Heap	P. Rosenthal, Esq.

Old City Hall
Courtroom M

CLERK OF THE COURT: Daniel Heap, Leonard Desroches and Robert Holmes, you are jointly charged on or about the second day of April in the year 1999, in the City of Toronto, in the Toronto Region, did commit mischief by wilfully attempting to remove a sword mounted on a war memorial without legal justification or excuse and without colour of right, the property of St. Paul's Anglican Church, situated at 227 Bloor Street East, the value of which exceeded five thousand dollars ($5,000.00) contrary to the Criminal Code.

On June 28, 1999 the Crown elected to proceed summarily. How do you speak to this charge, Daniel Heap, guilty or not guilty?

THE ACCUSED: Not guilty.

CLERK OF THE COURT: How do you plead to this charge, Leonard Desroches, guilty or not guilty?

THE ACCUSED: Not guilty.

CLERK OF THE COURT: And how do you plead to this charge, Robert Holmes, guilty or not guilty?

THE ACCUSED: Not guilty.

HARSTON FORDE: SWORN
EXAMINATION IN-CHIEF BY MR. CARRINGTON:

Q. As a member of St. Paul's Anglican Church, I understand you were called the People's Warden?

A. Yes, I am.

Q. Can you just explain what that title means, People's Warden?

A. A People's Warden of the Anglican Church is a position that is written in the laws of the Anglican Church. The People's Warden is responsible for the employees of the church, the property of the charge and he's charged with making sure that all the laws relating to these facets of the church are met, both in the church, the province and the national laws.

Q. Okay. Now, in your function as the People's Warden of St. Paul's Anglican church, prior to April 2nd, 1999, did you receive any communication from any of the three gentlemen that are seated before the Court here, Messieurs Heap, Holmes or Desroches and, if so, can you explain?

A. We had meetings with them in '97 and again we communicated with them in '98 prior to their...this proposed action. There was a meeting prior to the 1999 action at the diocese [where] the Corporation of St. Paul's and these three individuals were invited.

Q. ...What was the position of the church at the end of this meeting?

A. We don't think that we had persuaded them not to take the action that they had proposed. Consequently we realized that it was something bigger than just the three individuals. I don't believe we had a real physical problem with the three individuals because they were sincere in their communication to us and everything they said they were going to do, they did. They didn't do anything contrary to what they were saying. Our main problem was that they were allegating these problems to a wider community, thus, engaging a following that in our opinion might become uncontrollable.

> WE WHO ENGAGE IN NONVIOLENT DIRECT ACTION ARE NOT THE CREATORS OF TENSION. WE MERELY BRING TO THE SURFACE THE HIDDEN TENSION THAT IS ALREADY ALIVE. WE BRING IT OUT INTO THE OPEN WHERE IT CAN BE SEEN AND DEALT WITH. LIKE A BOIL THAT CAN NEVER BE CURED SO LONG AS IT IS COVERED…
> **Martin Luther King Jr.**

> WHEN THE BOIL HAS COME TO A HEAD IT MUST BE LANCED AND BURNED WITH FIRE. IF THAT IS NOT DONE AND ONLY A PLASTER PUT OVER IT, THE CORRUPTION WILL SPREAD AND THAT IS OFTEN WORSE THAN DEATH.
> **St. Catherine of Sienna**

> AS A CHRISTIAN, QUAKER, RELIGIOUS AND CONSCIENTIOUS OBJECTOR TO THE WHOLE INSTITUTION OF ORGANIZED WAR, I MUST HENCEFORTH REFUSE TO CONTRIBUTE TO IT IN ANY WAY I CAN AVOID.

Caroline Urie, bedridden and elderly, in a 1948 open letter to President Truman and the IRS explaining why she was withholding the 34.6 percent of her taxes used for war and donating the sum to four peace organizations.

Q. All right.

A. And consequently we had to contact Metro Police and tell them really, in our opinion, what was happening: the possibility that we might need some protection for our memorial...

Q. Okay. What's your recall of roughly how many police officers attended?

A. About 30.

Q. ...Now, these defendants, in all of their communications, stated that what they may do would be peaceful, is that not correct?

A. Well, they said what they were going to do, but they didn't say what the followers would do.

P.C. EVERETT ELLIOTT: SWORN
EXAMINATION IN-CHIEF BY MR. CARRINGTON:

Q. You were essentially a coordinating officer in attendance at St. Paul's Anglican Church at 227 Bloor Street East back on April 2nd, 1999, Good Friday?

> THIRTY TORONTO POLICE OFFICERS IN FULL RIOT GEAR—SUMMONED BY THE RECTOR AND WARDENS OF ST. PAUL'S—ARRESTED THE TRIO, TOOK THEM AWAY IN A PADDY WAGON...
> **Michael Valpy,** *The Globe and Mail,* May 29, 2000

A. Yes, sir.

Q. And your purpose in being there was that you had advance notice of a demonstration?

A. That's correct.

Q. All right. And I understand, sir, that you had some communication with members of St. Paul's Church?

A. Yes, I did.

Q. All right. And were you requested to perform any function by the church on behalf of the Toronto Police Service?

A. Yes. I spoke to Ms. Marlis Scott and she repeated what I had already understood to be the reason for the demonstration and then she both granted the permission and requested that myself and the other officers with me act as agents of the church in regards to trespass matters.

Q. Officer, there wasn't any threat to violence at any time, was there?

A. Not a… not a threat of violence to people, no; damage to the monument, that was all.

Q. Would you agree that even with people gathered that there was no hint or threat of violence?

A. That's correct.

Soldiers are refused entry into the refugee village of X'oyep by the women of Las Abejas (The Bees), an indigenous Christian pacifist group, in Chiapas, Mexico.

THOMAS GUMBLETON: SWORN
EXAMINATION IN-CHIEF BY MR. ROSENTHAL:

Q. Good morning, sir. I've addressed you as Bishop Gumbleton. Is that a correct form of address?

A. That's correct.

Q. Where are you a bishop?

A. In the Catholic Archdiocese of Detroit.

Q. And when were you appointed bishop, sir?

A. March 4th, 1968.

Q. And who appoints a person, a bishop, in the Catholic church?

A. The Pope, the Bishop of Rome.

Q. And can you roughly describe your duties from 1968 to present and what you've been doing as a bishop in Detroit?

A. My duties are comprised of pastoral care for the parishes throughout the archdiocese. I share in the administrative and pastoral responsibilities for the diocese.

I also have a specific pastoral charge of a parish in the city of Detroit and so I celebrate liturgies throughout the diocese, celebrate the sacrament of confirmation, do that sort of thing. And also oversee the work of the priests in the parishes.

> THE PASTORAL PLANNING OF THE CHURCH FOR THE NEW AGE OF THE THIRD MILLENNIUM NEEDS TO BE FOUNDED ON A NEW MATURE SPIRITUAL STRENGTH ADEQUATE FOR OUR AGE. THAT SPIRITUAL ENERGY IS THE POWER OF THE CROSS. [NONVIOLENT] MOVEMENTS MUST BE MADE STRUCTURAL AND CONTINUOUS PROCESSES, IN SEASON AND OUT OF SEASON. THE CHURCH IS CALLED TO OFFER THE INSPIRATION AND METHODOLOGY. [NONVIOLENCE] WILL BE THE HEALING PROCESS TO DRAW US TO RECONCILIATION AND TO THE GRACE OF THAT SACRAMENT.
>
> **Theotonius Gomes**, CSC, bishop of Dinajpur, Bangladesh, at a synod intervention (Rome, October 12, 1987)

Q. Now you have been in court this morning. You've heard the agreed statement of facts...

A. Yes.

Q. ...as to what the three accused persons did on the occasion of April 2nd, 1999, Good Friday?

A. Yes, I'm aware of that.

Q. And from your vantage point, sir, as a bishop, could you shed any light on any possible justification, as His Honour has indicated, that might be one of our main defences for those actions?

A. I think I might be able to. The placing of a sword in conjunction with the cross creates a very powerful symbol that is directly contrary to what would be the foundational teaching of Jesus Christ—so therefore the foundational teaching of the church, as a Christian community—and it creates this contradiction which goes against the very foundation and truth of the whole church. And coming from Jesus, who came and rejected violence of any kind whatsoever for any reason whatsoever, and who taught that we had to go even beyond the simple clear statement, "Thou shalt not kill," to the point of saying, "You may not even have hatred or violence in your heart, and if you do and you're going to offer your worship to God, you must leave the altar and go first and be reconciled." Never can you claim to be fully Christian and at the same time be committed to any sort of violence in your heart. The church must teach that and live that.

> GROW STRONG IN GOD, WITH THE STRENGTH OF GOD'S POWER. FOR IT IS NOT AGAINST HUMAN ENEMIES THAT WE HAVE TO STRUGGLE, BUT AGAINST THE PRINCIPALITIES AND POWERS.
> **Letter to the church community at Ephesus** (Eph. 6:10–12)

> WE CANNOT EMPHASIZE ENOUGH THE IMPORTANCE OF DEEP SPIRITUALITY. IT IS THIS WHICH GIVES PEOPLE THE STRENGTH TO STAND IN FRONT OF TANKS WHEN THE TIME COMES. IN A REVOLUTIONARY PROCESS, PEOPLE ARE HIGHLY EMOTIONAL. IT MAKES A DIFFERENCE WHETHER YOU PROMOTE HATRED AND REVENGE OR YOU HELP THE PEOPLE STAND FIRMLY FOR JUSTICE WITHOUT BECOMING LIKE THE OPPRESSOR. YOU WANT TO LOVE YOUR ENEMY, TO LIBERATE RATHER THAN DESTROY.
>
> **Hildegard Goss-Mayr** speaking of her experience in preparing people for the nonviolent overthrow of the Marcos military dictatorship in the Philippines in the mid 1980s

And so I would say putting a sword on a cross is contradictory—as if you were in Nazi Germany and they draped a flag over the cross with a swastika symbol. The two things are just basically contradictory and they cannot go together. The cross and the sword cannot go together and it's important to remove such symbols because symbols speak very powerfully to people. Especially—well, I shouldn't compare with other religious traditions—but I do know in the Christian tradition that we teach as much through symbol as we do through word. So that kind of symbol is telling people who come into that church are a message that is contrary to the message of Christ.

> I COMMIT MYSELF TO RESPECT FOR THE LIFE OF PERSONS AND PEOPLES, OF THE ANIMALS AND OF THE WHOLE OF CREATION. I COMMIT MYSELF TO BUILD PEACE EVERY DAY. I CHOOSE ACTIVE NONVIOLENCE AS A WAY OF LIFE.
>
> **Bishop Proano of Equador**, member of *Servicio Paz Y Justicia* (SERPAJ), the network of active nonviolence in Central and South America

Bishop Thomas Gumbleton of Detroit, Michigan, U.S.A.

THE COURT: Before we go any further, could you explain to me how the Catholic church could then justify Joan of Arc?

THE WITNESS: How it can justify what?

THE COURT: Justify Joan of Arc.

THE WITNESS: I don't believe it can justify Joan of Arc and be consistent with the teachings of the church itself. You know, Pope John Paul just recently made a very powerful statement, asking forgiveness for the times that the church has sinned in waging war like the Crusades.

> WE WANT, AS PASTORS OF THE CHURCH IN POLAND, TO STAND IN TRUTH BEFORE GOD AND PEOPLE, BUT MAINLY BEFORE OUR JEWISH BROTHERS AND SISTERS, REFERRING WITH REGRET AND REPENTANCE TO THE CRIME THAT IN JULY, 1941, TOOK PLACE IN JEDWABNE AND IN OTHER PLACES. **Poland's Roman Catholic bishops**, May 27, 2001, referring to the massacre of 1,600 Jews in Jedwabne by Poles, not Nazi troops

> I WANT TO MAKE A SPECIAL APPEAL TO SOLDIERS, NATIONAL GUARDSMEN, AND POLICEMEN: WHEN YOU HEAR THE WORDS OF A MAN TELLING YOU TO KILL, REMEMBER INSTEAD THE WORDS OF GOD, "YOU SHALL NOT KILL." GOD'S LAW MUST PREVAIL. NO SOLDIER IS OBLIGED TO OBEY AN ORDER CONTRARY TO THE LAW OF GOD. IT IS TIME THAT YOU COME TO YOUR SENSES AND OBEY YOUR CONSCIENCE RATHER THAN FOLLOW A SINFUL COMMAND.
> **Archbishop Oscar Romero**

> WE TALK ABOUT DEMOCRACY AND CHRISTIANITY—AND WE TRY OUT A NEW FIREBOMB. THIS COUNTRY HAS GONE MAD. BUT I WILL NOT GO MAD WITH IT. I WILL NOT PAY FOR ORGANIZED MURDER. **Joan Baez**, U.S. singer-songwriter, explaining her resistance to the Vietnam War

THE COURT: Yes.

THE WITNESS: …or the kind of thing that Joan of Arc did in waging war on behalf of the country of France at that time would not be consistent with what Jesus himself taught. And so there are times where the church fails in its living up to the teachings of Jesus, and that's because the church is made up of human beings. We sometimes are not able to live up to the full radical demands that the gospel makes. I think that's what was happening in this situation with people putting a sword on a cross

> NONVIOLENCE IS WRITTEN IN THE VERY HEART OF THE GOSPEL. **Général Jacques de Bollardiére**. After thirty years of active warfare and many military honours ("Grand Officier" of the "Légion d'Honneur"; "Compagnon de la liberation"; "Distinguished Service Order"; commander of the "Étoile noir"; recipient of both Belgium's and Holland's "Croix de guerre"), he completely renounced all war and converted to active nonviolence

THE COURT: But the church itself declared Joan of Arc a saint. A person to be followed, as a person who gives an example to Catholics.

THE WITNESS: But a person can be declared a saint who has sinned. Peter himself denied Jesus three times and yet he is held up as a saint and, you know, a model for Popes for all the centuries. And so the fact that a person has been declared a saint doesn't preclude that person as having committed grievous sins, even going so far so to betray or deny Jesus. So it's not a contradiction.

MR. ROSENTHAL:

Q. Thank you, sir. Now in addition to the effect that you mentioned, in your view would there be any concrete effects from a person trying to do something like remove the sword from the cross in this case?

A. I think it would teach a very powerful message if you could remove that sword. To me it would be similar to what Jesus did when he went into the temple area and knocked over the tables of the money changers and drove them out. He was teaching people in a very symbolic and powerful way, "Don't make God's house a den of thieves." That message came through very powerfully to the early Christian communities because you find it recorded in all four accounts of the gospel. So his symbolic action was very powerful and I think the same thing could be true here. This would speak a very powerful message that we need to reform within the church itself, and we need to declare it and live out our declaration that violence is not acceptable for a follower of Christ.

> ...OUR CHURCH IS IN NEED OF HEALING. WITHOUT THAT HEALING, WE WILL CONTINUE THE SAME ATTITUDES THAT HAVE DONE SUCH DAMAGE IN THE PAST... I ACCEPT AND I CONFESS BEFORE GOD AND YOU, OUR FAILURES IN THE RESIDENTIAL SCHOOLS. WE FAILED YOU. WE FAILED OURSELVES. WE FAILED GOD...I AM SORRY, MORE THAN I CAN SAY, THAT IN OUR SCHOOLS SO MANY WERE ABUSED PHYSICALLY, SEXUALLY, CULTURALLY AND EMOTIONALLY... LIFE AND WHOLENESS ARE THE EVERLASTING AND UNQUENCHABLE PURPOSE OF GOD.
>
> Canadian Anglican Primate, **Archbishop Michael Peers**, to the National Native Convocation, Minaki, Ontario, August 6, 1993

Q. Now, are you aware of any similar activities in the United States, for example, to what these persons did on this occasion?

A. Yes. And not only in the United States, throughout the world, there are actions of this sort that have been carried in dramatic and prophetic ways, to try to call people back to the radical teachings of the gospel of Jesus. Now, I know of actions like this in the United Kingdom, in the United States, in Mexico, in various parts of Latin America and Central America. I've been involved in such actions myself in other places in order to do this very same thing.

> OUR MORAL, POLITICAL AND ECONOMIC RESPONSIBILITIES DO NOT STOP AT BIRTH. THOSE WHO DEFEND THE RIGHT TO LIFE OF THE WEAKEST AMONG US MUST BE EQUALLY VISIBLE IN SUPPORT OF THE QUALITY OF LIFE OF THE POWERLESS AMONG US. **Cardinal Joseph**

Bernardin (RC), U.S.A., referring to the *Seamless Garment* ethic which he helped shape

Q. Now when you've been involved in such actions, would you have any aspirations to actually affect events in a short term sense as well as express your theological view?

A. Well, where I've been involved generally there has not been an immediate short term effect. What we're trying to do is to teach people that in spite of the fact that you're arrested and you perhaps are put in jail, and so in a sense your action fails, you haven't really changed anything immediately, but your witness helps to build up a mentality within the church and beyond the church that the kinds of things that you're acting against are wrong. Especially when people are willing to spend time in jail, I think it authenticates their witness, because it shows that it's not self-serving. They are doing it for the greater good.

> AS A VETERAN OF THE VIETNAM WAR I CANNOT HELP BUT CRY OUT BELATEDLY, IN AN ACT OF ATONEMENT, AGAINST THE MARTIAL MENTALITY WHICH JUSTIFIES WARMAKING AS A MEANS OF RESOLVING HUMAN CONFLICT AND DIFFERENCES. AS A HUSBAND AND AS A FATHER OF THREE BEAUTIFUL, LOVING DAUGHTERS I CANNOT HELP BUT PERSEVERE IN MY PROTEST AT AN INSTITUTION [THE PENTAGON] WHICH GENERATES FEAR, HATRED AND VIOLENCE.
> **Peter De Mott**, Ithaca, NY

> WE DID THE JOB. NONE OF THE IRAQI VEHICLES FIRED BACK. ALL WERE DESTROYED. THERE WERE NO SURVIVORS. COMBAT WAS GREAT—THERE JUST WASN'T ENOUGH OF IT. I DON'T ENVY THE PEOPLE WHO DIDN'T GET TO EXPERIENCE THIS.
> U.S. Staff Sgt. **Carlton Jones** in *Context*, July 15, 1991

CROSS EXAMINATION BY MR. SALVATERRA:

Q. Given the kind of proceedings I'm not so sure I'll be quite as kind, but I'll nevertheless ask a few questions if I may. Bishop Gumbleton, do you have any personal knowledge of any of these defendants?

A. Well, I've known Robert Holmes for probably 30 years, 31 years, I think back to about 1969. He worked as a priest in the archdiocese of Detroit and so I knew him back then. I've had personal contact with him, well, quite a bit during those years when he was in Detroit, from '69 to '79, and then off and on since. And Leonard Desroches I've known only mostly through correspondence and telephone conversations. And Heap I don't know, I have not met until last night.

Q. In answer to one question about the contradiction of the sword and cross, it was like putting a swastika over a Jewish symbol like a menorah or a Star of David?

A. Yes, it would be like that. The inherent contradiction is just very, very clear.

Q. And what, in your view, does removing a cross, a sword from a cross, accomplish?

A. It clears the symbol to say what it's supposed to say. The cross speaks of non-violence and forgiveness, even of the ones who are putting you to death. So the cross is a very powerful message in itself. It sums up the whole message of Jesus. That you don't conquer through power of force or coercion, but you transform through love. That's what the cross says. And so once you remove that sword the cross can speak the powerful message that it's intended to speak.

AND YOU…MY LAST MINUTE FRIEND, WHO COULD NOT HAVE KNOWN WHAT YOU WERE DOING, YES, FOR YOU TOO, I SAY… "A-DIEU"—TO COMMEND YOU TO THE GOD IN WHOSE FACE I SEE YOURS. AMEN! INSHA'ALLAH!

Testament of **Christian De Chergé**, Cistercian monk, addressing the fundamentalist extremists who eventually killed him, May 21, 1996

Q. And having the sword on a cross what, in your view, is the message that that sends?

A. It's a message that then nonviolence of Jesus isn't enough. We have to bring human violence into it and that's totally wrong. I mean, the message of Jesus is that we transform this world, that we transform violent situations by bringing acts of love into those situations and the sword can add nothing to that. It only detracts and contradicts.

> I WAS ABDUCTED FROM THE BACK YARD OF THE POSADA DE BELEN RETREAT CENTER IN ANTIGUA BY MEMBERS OF THE GUATEMALAN SECURITY FORCES. THEY TOOK ME TO A CLANDESTINE PRISON WHERE I WAS TORTURED AND RAPED REPEATEDLY. MY BACK AND CHEST WERE BURNED MORE THAN 111 TIMES WITH CIGARETTES. I WAS LOWERED INTO AN OPEN PIT PACKED WITH HUMAN BODIES—BODIES OF CHILDREN, WOMEN, AND MEN, SOME DECAPITATED, SOME LYING FACE UP AND CAKED WITH BLOOD, SOME DEAD, SOME ALIVE—AND ALL SWARMING WITH RATS.

Diana Ortiz, U.S. Ursuline nun who worked in San Miguel Acatan, a poor, rural area of Guatemala, teaching Mayan children to read, write and reflect on the Bible in the context of their Mayan culture

> WE WANT THIS SCHOOL [OF THE AMERICAS] CLOSED BECAUSE IT IS A SCHOOL OF THUGS. IT IS A SCHOOL OF TERRORISTS.

Roy Bourgeois, *The Truth Cannot Be Silence—The Trial Testimonies of the "SOA 13"*. Roy is a Maryknoll priest who worked in the slums on the outskirts of La Paz, Bolivia during the brutal dictator ship of SOA-graduate Hugo Banzer Suarez. After visiting the prisons and seeing widespread evidence of torture, he spoke out against the dictatorship during a visit to the United States. The Bolivian authorities prevented his return. He has since helped to found the *SOA Watch*, a group which has exposed the atrocities taught at the *School of the Americas* at Fort Benning, Georgia, U.S.A.

Q. Now this was a public monument. Would you agree with me that that monument, then, is making a public statement?
A. Yes, of course.
MR. SALVATERRA:
Q. And your understanding of the word blasphemy, if I may?
A. My understanding of the word blasphemy would be that you place someone else in the place of God or some other thing in the place of God and so it's like creating an idol that you worship instead of the true God.

> THROUGH THE CROSS JESUS ENTERED INTO THE CRUCIFIXION OF THE WORLD. IN DOING SO, HE REVEALED THE OTHER SIDE OF VIOLENCE, WHICH IS SUFFERING, AS A WAY OF RESISTANCE—A WAY OF TRANSFORMING VIOLENCE INTO LIFE ITSELF.
> **Jim Douglass**, *The Nonviolent Coming of God*

> WE SHALL MAKE SURE THAT OUR ADVERSARIES
> SHALL NEVER RISE AGAIN
> NOT IN THREE DAYS—NOR EVER
> FOR WE ARE AN EASTER PEOPLE
> AND OUR SONG IS ALLELUIA
> **Ann Fremantle**, from the poem *No Mindless Escalation*

Q. Now the cross is a symbol of God, of the Christ, is it not?
A. Yes, because it's clearly the symbol of Jesus and carries the very powerful message of Jesus and so to do something that substitutes another message is a kind of blasphemy.

> THE NONVIOLENT ALTERNATIVE WILL SURELY LEAD US TO GO BEYOND THE CONCEPT OF THE "JUST WAR", IN ORDER TO DARE MOVE TOWARDS THE BIBLICAL SOLUTIONS OF FORGIVENESS OF SINS, LOVE OF THE ENEMY, AND RESOLUTION OF CONFLICTS IN TRUTH AND TOTAL RESPECT

FOR THE HUMAN PERSON. **Joseph Beaulieu**, former captain in the Canadian Armed Forces

Q. Thank you. Now what, in your view, has this Just War Doctrine justified in today's circumstances of war?

A. By having a teaching justifying use of violence we have opened the way to what we now call in human history "total war," where the majority of people who die in war are non-combatants, innocent civilians. [In] the wars of this century, an even greater percentage of people who have been killed have not been in the military but innocent civilians. And so…all [of this] flows out of saying that there are times you can justify the use of violence. In the history of warfare, we have constantly justified the use of violence, and it becomes greater and greater and greater.

> THOSE WHO GO TO EGYPT FOR HELP ARE DOOMED, RELYING ON EGYPT'S VAST MILITARY STRENGTH.
>
> YOUR STRENGTH LAY IN COMPLETE TRUST.
> **Isaiah** (31:1; 30:15)
>
> CAN WE CONCEIVE OF BEING FOREVER CONDEMNED TO MAKE WAR? **Adolphe Proulx**, late Catholic bishop of Gatineau-Hull
>
> WAR NOW DEPENDS MORE ON MONEY THAN ON PERSONNEL; IT ONLY TOOK TWELVE MEN TO DROP THE BOMB OVER HIROSHIMA, BUT IT TOOK MILLIONS, PERHAPS BILLIONS, OF TAXPAYERS' DOLLARS IN CANADA, BRITAIN AND THE UNITED STATES TO DEVELOP THAT BOMB.
>
> **Edith Adamson**, in a 1982 statement explaining why she became the coordinator of the Peace Tax Fund Committee of Canada

A. And even a so-called conventional war can lead to a violence that's in a sense almost out of control. And then beyond that we even justify the use of weapons of mass destruction by having this kind of a theology. And so in its very root it's wrong because it leads to consequences that defy any human acceptability.

> THE ESSENTIAL THING FOR US IS TO DESTROY THE IMAGE OF THE ENEMY WHICH IS IMPOSED ON US. **The Group for the Establishment of Trust Between the East and the West, Moscow, during the Cold War**

Q. What, in your knowledge, are some of these [immediate] consequences today?

A. Well, I think that we have the world right now under the threat of immediate destruction. You have 35,000 nuclear weapons in the world—5,000 of those are on active alert at this very moment. In a matter of 15 minutes to a half hour, the world would be gone, because we have justified the use of violence. Not only is that absolutely immoral, it's just absurd. It goes against even human reason to justify that kind of violence. And that, too, is a kind of blasphemy. We're saying to God, "We can destroy everything you have made." You're acting against the very creative power of God's love when you deploy nuclear weapons and intend to use them and, in fact, do use them.

> AT LEAST 30.4 MILLION FATALITIES AND SERIOUS INJURIES ARE ATTRIBUTABLE TO NUCLEAR ACTIVITIES, 1943 TO 1990.
>
> **Rosalie Bertell**, GNSH, President of the International Institute of Public Concern and President of the North American Association of Contemplative Sisters

So that's probably the worst blasphemy that could ever happen and it all flows from justifying the use of violence. And that's why Jesus said, "No, never violence." That's why Pope John Paul II, a few years ago, in a statement said, "Violence is a lie. Violence is not the Christian way. Violence is not the way of the Catholic church. Do not believe in violence. Do not use violence. Peace, forgiveness and love, these are the way of Christ," and that's all. Violence is out.

DO NOT FEED YOUR SPIRIT ON ANYTHING APART FROM GOD. CAST AWAY ALL CARES AND LET PEACE AND RECONCILIATION FILL YOUR HEART.

St. John of the Cross, arrested and imprisoned by church officials for his radical reformations

MR. SALVATERRA:

Q. Beyond message, if I might ask, do you believe that removing the cross from the sword would save lives, any life?

A. Ultimately it would, I believe.

Q. How so?

A. By reversing this tendency to justify the use of violence. It would be a first step in that direction and every step we can take in that direction will save lives.

Q. Would it be necessary then, in your view, to commence the saving of lives at least through an action like this?

A. Yes, I think it would be necessary.

THE COURT: Isn't there a bit of a contradiction here? We start with the premise that there should be peace. There should be no violence whatsoever. Yet we have three persons here who trespass on a property after being told, "Do not do that," and then the intention is to go and damage the property. Isn't that the beginning of violence, imposing your views on somebody else by physical actions?

THE WITNESS: First of all, the action is an action against property, which is very different from an action against people. If I were living in the time of World War II which I did live in—I was a child at the time, though—and I had an opportunity to destroy a crematorium in Auschwitz, I think I would have an obligation to do that. If I had an opportunity to try to prevent the cattle cars carrying prisoners from Germany and France and all over Europe to Auschwitz or any of the death camps, I think I would have a responsibility to damage those cattle cars in whatever way I could so that they could not be used.

WE STRUGGLE BY RENDERING OPERATIVE THE FORCE OF LOVE IN THE BATTLE OF LIBERATION. ACTIVE NONVIOLENCE IS A RESPONSE THAT

IS BASED ON THE GOSPEL. IT IS A SPIRIT AND A METHOD. IT IS A SPIRIT OF PROPHECY, FOR IT DENOUNCES ALL SUNDERING OF A COMMUNITY OF BROTHERS AND SISTERS AND PROCLAIMS THAT THIS COMMUNITY CAN ONLY BE REBUILT THROUGH LOVE. AND IT IS A METHOD—AN ORGANIZED SET OF RUPTURES IN THE CIVIL ORDER SO AS TO DISTURB THE SYSTEM RESPONSIBLE FOR THE INJUSTICES WE SEE AROUND US. THE MEANS WILL INCLUDE BOYCOTTS, STRIKES, NON-COOPERATION, CIVIL DISOBEDIENCE, HUNGER STRIKES, AND MANY OTHER ACTIONS. **Adolfo Perez Esquivel**, Nobel Prize laureate who was arrested and tortured for his public denunciation of the Argentinian dictatorship and for his support of the "Mothers of the Plaza De Mayo—the Mothers of the Disappeared"

And I don't think that that is violence. To me that's much more like Jesus knocking over the tables in the temple. That's not doing violence against any person. You're trying to show that property can be misused and it may not be misused in that way, and so you prevent it by destroying the property.

MASTERS OF SPACE
Publicity mantra of the U.S. Space Command

WE REJECT THE VISION OF THE [U.S.] SPACE COMMAND THAT "THE WAY A NATION MAKES WEALTH IS THE WAY IT MAKES WAR." WE REJECT THAT THE UNITED STATES MUST CONTROL SPACE "AS CRITICAL TO BOTH MILITARY AND ECONOMIC INSTRUMENTS OF POWER—THE MAIN SOURCES OF NATIONAL STRENGTH." **Carol Gilbert**, OP; **Jackie Hudson**, OP; **Anne Montgomery**, RSCJ; **Ardeth Platte**, OP; **Liz Walters**, IHM—*Sacred Earth and Space Plowshares 2000*

> SPACE SOON WILL BE THE FOURTH MEDIUM OF WARFARE. IT WILL NOT ONLY BIND ALL WAR FIGHTING FORCES TOGETHER BUT WILL ALSO BECOME STRATEGICALLY CRITICAL TO THE SURVIVAL OF WARFIGHTERS…FOR FUTURE COALITION WARFARE, SPACE SUPERIORITY WILL BE FUNDAMENTAL.
>
> **Canadian government technology investment strategy**, part of War Research and Development Canada 2000

THE COURT: But interfering with somebody else's property, is it not a manifestation of violence?

THE WITNESS: Well, here again I think we're talking in terms of symbol to a certain extent and symbols speak very powerfully. The message that you're trying to give here is a message that Christians are called to give one another, what in the scriptures is called correcting your brothers or sisters when they have fallen into evil. And so we're bound to try to do brotherly or sisterly correction. And I think that's what the action is in this case. It's a way of speaking to the church and saying, "We may not do this and we're calling one another to authentically following the way of Jesus."

> PREACHING THAT DOESN'T DENOUNCE SIN IS NOT PREACHING THE GOSPEL **Archbishop Oscar Romero**

MR. SALVATERRA:

Q. Just arising from that, if I may, just one further question. With respect to damage to property versus damage to human beings, contravening property versus contravening human life, do you put those on equal levels?

A. No, absolutely not. Property does not have rights. Human persons have rights.

ALL THE CONFLICTS THAT I KNOW OF AT THE POLITICAL LEVEL ALWAYS HAVE THE SAME DYNAMIC THAT IS BETWEEN MYSELF AND THE HANDICAPPED PERSON: IN MY WILL TO CONTROL THAT PERSON, TERRIBLE VIOLENCE CAN OCCUR.
Jean Vanier, founder of l'Arche. Jean served in the British and Canadian navies in the Second World War before resigning his commission in 1950

Q. What is the foundation of your understanding?
A. The rights of a human person. The fact that we are made in the image and likeness of God gives us an inherent dignity that enables us or that gives us the right to full development as a human person to become as perfect an image of God as possible. So we have the right to that full development as a person. Every person on this earth has that same basic dignity and the rights that flow from that dignity of being created in the image of God.

IF WE HAVE TO USE [MILITARY] FORCE, IT IS BECAUSE WE ARE AMERICA. WE ARE THE INDISPENSABLE NATION. WE STAND TALL. WE SEE FURTHER INTO THE FUTURE.

Madeline Albright, former U.S. Secretary of State in the Clinton administration

SEPTEMBER 11 CHANGED THE WORLD. YET I AM CONVINCED THAT MILITARY ACTION WILL NOT PREVENT FURTHER ACTS OF INTERNATIONAL TERRORISM. OUR GREATEST MEMORIAL TO OUR FALLEN BROTHERS AND SISTERS WILL BE A WORLD OF PEACE, TOLERANCE AND UNDERSTANDING. LET US NOT BECOME THE EVIL THAT WE DEPLORE.

Barbara Lee, U.S. Congresswoman (D, CA) who cast the lone vote 9/14/01 against President Bush's resolution calling for military force

HAVE WE FORGOTTEN THAT WE ARE ALL MEMBERS OF ONE ANOTHER?
St. Clement

REMEMBER THAT OUR COUNTRY IS PART OF THE WHOLE.

Amber Amundson, whose husband, Craig Scott Amundson, perished September 11. Amber remains committed to nonviolent alternatives to war

Q. One further question. Would you agree with me that the source of property is God created?
A. Well, the source of the whole universe is God, so, yes.
Q. Thank you. Nothing further.
MR. CARRINGTON: I have no further questions.
THE COURT: Thank you, sir. Thank you.
THE WITNESS: Thank you.

JANET SOMERVILLE: SWORN
EXAMINATION IN-CHIEF BY MR. ROSENTHAL:

Q. I'm not sure if it's still quite good morning, but greetings. Ms. Somerville, can you tell us what your occupation is?
A. I'm the general secretary of the Canadian Council of Churches.
Q. And what is the Canadian Council of Churches, briefly?
A. It's a forum of churches, a network of churches, including all of the major large churches in Canada and several smaller churches, 19 member churches in all, through which they meet together to understand each other more deeply; to cooperate on actions on which they agree and to grow toward closer unity.

WHO WILL SEPARATE US FROM THE LOVE OF CHRIST? WILL HARDSHIP, OR DISTRESS, OR PERSECUTION OR FAMINE OR NAKEDNESS OR PERIL OR SWORD?

Letter to the church community in Rome (Romans 8:35)

Q. And you've told us you are the executive director of that organization?

A. Yes. The title is general secretary but it's the same animal.

Q. And just briefly, what are your responsibilities in that position, ma'am?

A. I wish the title were something like web mistress, because the essence of the job is helping the churches to remain in conversation with each other across the country.

Q. Now in that position it's important for you to be aware of what's happening in the Christian world in Canada?

A. It is.

Q. Now, you've heard the evidence so far in this case?

A. M'hmm.

Q. I understand that you were present on April 2nd, 1999, is that correct?

A. I was.

Q. And you witnessed the events that were described here?

A. That's true.

Q. What was your view in attending those events?

A. It was, for me, part of my prayer on Good Friday, because every Good Friday in Toronto there is a large ecumenical gathering of people who remember the circumstances of the death of Jesus in terms of injustices being suffered now by the poor and by minorities and by other people that we tend to be hard on. And this was the final event of that ecumenical prayerful gathering that day. So for me it was a continuation of my own prayer.

DON'T JUST DO SOMETHING, STAND THERE.
Daniel Berrigan

Janet Somerville, General Secretary of the Canadian Council of Churches

I have known Len and Dan Heap since about 1970. I've known Bob Holmes less long, but I've known his religious community since I was a little child and I have found them challenging witnesses to the more radical side of the gospel all my life. My temperament and my job incline me more to the middle ground where you listen to both sides and struggle to see which way the wind of the Spirit is blowing. It seems to be that although most people who go to church still agree with something like the Doctrine of the Just War, the direction that the spirit is blowing in is toward a more radical and deeper understanding, that [the Just War Doctrine} is not a Christian option.

> THE MAINLINE CHURCHES NEED TO STRETCH THEIR IMAGINATION TO DEVELOP AND CULTIVATE THE CONCEPT OF NONVIOLENCE AND A MORE POSITIVE APPROACH TO PACIFISM.
>
> **Dr. Milan Opocensky**, Czech theologian, General Secretary of the *World Alliance of Reformed Churches*, reflecting on NATO's military involvement in Yugoslavia

Q. And is that your personal view then?

A. I have been struggling all my life with this. I did my M.A. thesis on this question—well, on the contrast between two particular popes on this question—and I have been struggling all my life with it. I don't think there is a rational way to finally answer the question, but I believe that I am being drawn by God toward an understanding that to live deeply the discipleship of Jesus does rule out violence. I still can't imagine how the world can be that way but I feel the pulling of the scripture in that direction for me.

> WE ARE CONVINCED THAT AT NO POINT HAS CHRISTENDOM DEPARTED SO RADICALLY FROM THE MIND OF CHRIST AND ITS OWN ORIGINAL FAITH AS IN ITS ACCEPTANCE OF WAR.
>
> ***A Witness Against War*** (October, 1939) a public statement of noncooperation with Canada's declaration of war, signed by 75 United Church ministers—some of whom lost their charges due to pressure from wealthy parishioners

THE COURT: I'm having trouble trying to follow what is going on here.

MR. ROSENTHAL: Yes.

THE COURT: Because it seems to be strictly a theological discussion.

MR. ROSENTHAL: Yes.

THE COURT: And as you know, that's not my role.

MR. ROSENTHAL: Yes, sir. Well, perhaps I could assist you by a little bit further explanation as to how the theological aspects do relate to what you have to decide, namely whether or not there is a justification. One aspect would be if, indeed, the presence of the sword on the cross is blasphemous, then it might be a question as to whether an attempt to remove it was or was not mischief.

> IF YOU LOOK TO THE LAW TO MAKE YOU JUSTIFIED, THEN YOU HAVE SEPARATED YOURSELVES FROM CHRIST. WHAT MATTERS IS FAITH THAT MAKES ITS POWER FELT THROUGH LOVE.

Letter to the early church community in Galatia (Gal. 5:4–6)

WE HAVE AVAILABLE TO US THE GREATEST RENEWABLE SOURCE OF POWER, PERHAPS THE ONLY ONE WHICH IS INCREASED THE MORE WE USE IT. **Jo Vellacott** in a 1981 essay "Women, Peace and Power"

THE COURT: Okay. That I can understand.
MR. ROSENTHAL: And so that's one aspect.
THE COURT: Okay.
MR. ROSENTHAL: Another aspect would be that if their attempt, as admitted, actually was to try to stop a war and had a realistic potential of beginning a discourse in that direction, and if they honestly believed that it would help save lives, even in the short run perhaps, and that the presence of a sword on a cross and the related notion that war is acceptable in Christianity…if we can persuade Your Honour that, in fact, is something they believed in and that it was reasonable for them to believe, and that that, in itself, kills people. Is killing…
THE COURT: Well, okay. Why don't you put the questions directly to Ms. Somerville, in that…
MR. ROSENTHAL: As to the action that these people took that day that you observed, is there any justification for that kind of behaviour and, if so, what, in your opinion?
A. In terms of life in the church—and this is a cross owned by a church, and the action took place on church property—in terms of life in the church, if I can say this as a church person, it certainly wasn't mischief and it didn't disrupt the life of the church. It is the life of the church. This is what we talk about all the time. This is a mainstream, central, worrisome, agonizing problem in the life of the church, and they were joining peacefully in a conversation that is central to the development of the conscience of the church right now in Canada in the beginning of the 21st century.

POWER BASED ON GUNS WILL NOT ENDURE. TO BRAVE THE CENTURIES, WE MUST INVADE AND

CONQUER THE SOUL. **Joseph Goebbels**, Minister of Propaganda for the Nazi government

NO NATION IS BLACK OR WHITE, BUT ALL SHARE IN RESPONSIBILITY FOR CREATING THE SITUATION WHICH MAKES WAR INEVITABLE. WAR IS FUTILE BECAUSE INCAPABLE OF ACHIEVING ANY WORTHY SOLUTION OF INTERNATIONAL DISPUTES.
A Witness Against War, 1939

It seems to me that although most people who go to church still agree with something like the Just War doctrine, the Spirit is blowing in another direction: towards a more radical and deeper understanding that war is not a Christian option...

I have been struggling all my life with this. I don't think there is a rational way to finally answer the question. But I believe I am being drawn by God towards an understanding that life as a disciple of Jesus does rule out violence. I still can't imagine how the world can actually be that way, but I feel scripture pulling in that direction for me...

In terms of life in the church... it certainly wasn't mischief and it didn't disrupt the life of the church: It <u>is</u> the life of the church.

> The placing of a sword in conjunction with the cross creates a very powerful symbol that is directly contrary to what would be the foundational teaching of Jesus Christ.
>
> The very foundation and truth of the whole Church
>
> It's important to remove such symbols because symbols speak very powerfully to people
>
> I think it would teach a very powerful message if you could remove that sword.
>
> This would speak a very powerful message that we need to reform within the Church itself, and we need to declare it and live out our declaration that violence is not acceptable for a follower of Jesus Christ
>
> once you remove that sword the cross can speak the powerful message that it's intended to speak.

Q. And is that why you attended?
A. Yes.
Q. To be…
A. Also to pray.

> PRAYER IS NOT AN ACCUMULATION OF SPIRITUAL KNOWLEDGE BUT A CAPACITY TO FACE THE SACRED MOMENT.
> **Rabbi Abraham Heschel**

Q. And to be part of that discussion?
A. To be part of that discussion…because I also have the deepest respect for the sentiments of people on the other side—like most members of my own family, for example, who were very disturbed by something

that could seem to deny the utter sincerity of many people who have given their lives in war, and who have killed in war.

> CHRIST'S PRECEPT "DO NOT JUDGE" SEEMS TO ME ESSENTIAL. MY PRESENT NONVIOLENT COMBAT HAS CAUSED ME OPPOSITION FROM EVEN THOSE WHO ARE APPARENTLY CLOSE TO ME. WHEN I SAW IN ALGERIA FRENCH OFFICERS DO WHAT THE NAZIS HAD DONE, I ASKED MYSELF IF I WAS CERTAIN OF BEING ALWAYS FREE OF SUCH ATTITUDES. WE CAN JUDGE THE SITUATIONS, BUT NOT THE PERSONS.
> **Général Jacques de Bollardiére**

Q. Now I had suggested to His Honour that, from a Christian point of view, the attempt to remove that cross might enhance the value of that monument as a Christian symbol rather than detract from it.

A. Yeah.

Q. What would your view be?

A. I think it would enhance it tremendously. I think it would. I agree with Bishop Gumbleton that it clarifies the symbol. I think that St. Paul's Church would be more of a magnet to people. I think it would have been understood and dealt with positively by the Christian population as a whole, even though not everyone would agree, of course. I think, yes, it would enhance the monument.

> WHAT IF, WE ASK, CANADA WERE TO LEAD THE WAY IN A MASSIVE EFFORT TO PROVIDE MEDICINE AND FOOD FOR THE SICK AND STARVING PEOPLE OF IRAQ? MIGHT THIS COUNTERACT THE PERCEPTION OF THE WEST AS THE ENEMY OF THE IRAQI PEOPLE AND POINT THE WAY FORWARD TO NEW POSSIBILITIES? MIGHT IT BUY TIME AND GOOD WILL FOR MORE INTENSE EFFORTS OF DIPLOMACY TO BEAR FRUIT?

Open letter to the prime minister concerning the possibility of an intervention in Iraq, signed by over 30 individuals and leaders from several faith communities in Canada—February 20, 1998

Q. Okay.

A. Both in a Christian sense and in a sense of attracting persons to that church.

Q. And what about affecting the discourse and affecting actual lives lost in war? Is there any potential for such actions?

A. Affecting the discourse, yes, because the discourse is so alive right now [that] a symbolic moment like this is the right time for it to pass from simply an academic verbal kind of discussion, to a discussion closer to the heart. Saving lives, that's much more indirect.

Q. Now, we almost missed your presence here because you expected to be far away from here today. What mission were you going on and how does that relate to these issues?

A. Archbishop Barry Curtis, the outgoing president of the Canadian Council of Churches, and I should have been co-chairing an ecumenical delegation in Iraq at this time. Seeing for ourselves the impact of the sanctions in an attempt to join, as concretely as possible, the many, many voices in the world, both of religious people and others, who are saying that those sanctions are now completely unjustifiable in terms of their impact on human life.

EPIDEMICS RAGE, TAKING AWAY INFANTS AND SICK BY THE THOUSANDS. THOSE CHILDREN WHO SURVIVE DISEASE SUCCUMB TO MALNUTRITION, WHICH STUNTS THEIR PHYSICAL AND MENTAL DEVELOPMENT. OUR SITUATION IS UNBEARABLE! **Archbishop Gabriel Kassab**, Iraq

MAINTAINING SUCH ECONOMIC SANCTIONS WITHOUT TIME CONSTRAINTS IS NOW AIMED MORE AT PROTECTING PARTICULAR INTERESTS THAN RE-ESTABLISHING THE PEACE AND SECURITY OF THE POPULATIONS

CONCERNED. FURTHERMORE, IT CONTRIBUTES TO MAINTAINING A CLIMATE OF VIOLENCE IN THE INTERNATIONAL COMMUNITY.

From the General Chapter of the Dominican Friars gathered in Providence, R.I., U.S.A. from July 9 to August 8, 2001.

Q. And what is your understanding of that impact, briefly?
A. That it is killing people and that the United Nations is being drawn by its complicity in those sanctions into the style of an old empire and not the style of the post-war world which we are trying to build.

WE SIMPLY REJECT THE GOVERNMENT'S CONTENTION THAT WE CANNOT CARRY MEDICINE TO THE SICK, AND ASSERT THAT IT IS A GREATER EVIL TO LET THE CHILDREN DIE. ECONOMIC WARFARE IS ACTUALLY MORE LETHAL, MORE BRUTAL AND MORE DEVASTATING THAN A LOT OF BOMBARDMENT THAT WE'VE SEEN, EVEN THE BOMBARDMENT IN THE GULF WAR.

Kathy Kelly, of *Voices in the Wilderness*, in response to a threat of a $163,000 fine by the U.S. Treasury Department

WHY ARE YOU KILLING US? **A group of Iraqi schoolgirls** to an F.O.R. delegation in the Spring of 1999

ELIZABETH LOUGHREY: SWORN
EXAMINATION IN-CHIEF BY MR. ROSENTHAL:

Q. Greetings. You are Reverend Loughrey, is that title correct?
A. Yes
Q. And by virtue of what position?
A. I am the priest to the congregation and community at All Saints Church Community Centre which is an Anglican outreach ministry at the intersection of Dundas and Sherbourne Streets.

Q. I see. And it's only recently that women were able to be ordained as priests in the Anglican faith, is that fair?

A. Some time later than the birth of Bishop Gumbleton, but, yes.

Q. When were you ordained?

A. I was ordained eleven years ago.

Q. And just briefly, could you tell us about your work in that parish?

A. Yes. Ours is not a self-sufficient parish. It was established as a parish 25 years ago. It is a mission of the Community Ministries Board of the Anglican Diocese of Toronto. Which means that our funding and our direction comes from Community Ministries. We have a small congregation in a very large space. As well as a small worshipping congregation our space is [also] used by other groups for community programming, which includes such essential services as health care, identification clinics, mail services and advocacy and referral work.

Rev. Jeannie Loughrey of All Saints Anglican Church, Toronto, with a friend

IF WE WANTED TO POSSESS ANYTHING, THEN WE WOULD ALSO NEED ARMS TO DEFEND OURSELVES. THAT IS HOW ALL THE QUARRELS AND CONFLICTS GET STARTED, AND THEY ARE AN OBSTACLE TO LOVE.
St. Francis of Assisi to his bishop

WAR IS A LICENSE TO KILL AND STEAL. PEOPLE LOSE THEIR SOULS IN WAR, THEY LOST THEIR LIVES AND THEIR LIVELIHOOD. **Bartolomé de las Casas**, 16th century Dominican bishop who dedicated his life to defending the first nations people of the Americas against the violent greed of his fellow Spaniards.

IN OUR CONSUMER SOCIETY WE CAN OBSERVE A VERY CLEAR TENDENCY TOWARDS THE PROLIFERATION OF ARMS. THERE IS A SORT OF MADNESS, A HYSTERIA WHICH MAKES US CONTINUE TO ARM OURSELVES TO THE DETRIMENT OF PEOPLES' ESSENTIAL NEEDS. **Bishop Adolphe Proulx**

THE ACID TEST IS NOT, "WILL YOU DIE FOR YOUR FAITH?" BUT, "WILL YOU CHEERFULLY SUFFER FINANCIAL LOSS FOR IT?"

Edis Fairbairn, pacifist and United Church minister in the *United Church Observer*, February 1, 1941. Fairbairn was officially rebuked and ejected from his church in Bracebridge, Ontario

WE STARTED QUESTIONING THE DESIGNING OF WEAPONS AS THE SOURCE OF OUR BREAD AND BUTTER. OUR INVOLVEMENT WITH THOSE WHO WERE PUTTING THEIR LIVES ON THE LINE FOR PEACE AND JUSTICE GAVE US THE COURAGE TO DISENGAGE OURSELVES FROM WEAPONS PRODUCTION.

Bob Aldridge, formerly a highly-paid designer of U.S. nuclear weapons. He, his wife, Janet, and their children accepted a whole different economic lifestyle as the cost of radical nonviolence

THE WARS GO ON IN OTHER QUARTERS OF THE GLOBE AND WE, AS THE RICHES NATION MAKING SO MUCH MONEY OUT OF OUR ARMAMENTS, ARE STILL VERY MUCH INVOLVED.

THERE MAY BE EVER-IMPROVING STANDARDS OF LIVING IN THE UNITED STATES, WITH EVERY WORKER EVENTUALLY OWNING HIS OWN HOME AND DRIVING HIS OWN CAR; BUT OUR WHOLE MODERN ECONOMY IS BASED ON PREPARATION FOR WAR, AND THIS SURELY IS ONE OF THE GREAT ARGUMENTS FOR POVERTY IN OUR TIME. **Dorothy Day**

> Previously the issue, for me, was largely an abstract symbol and therefore, did not command much attention. But living in the inner city, as I do, in a conflicted neighbourhood, as I do, the reality of violence at all levels has become much more real for me.
>
> When Jesus was in the garden on the evening of this arrest, when he was confronted by soldiers, he neither fought them nor did he flee, but instead he stood in active testimony to the truth that he carried, and that is a reality that has become more real for me. It is a reality which precludes violence for violence is a diminishment of other human beings and that the call for truth living that God places upon each one of us.
>
> The cross is a central symbol of Christianity. It is, above all, a symbol of redemptive love. That kind of love affords no opportunity for violence. The imposition of an instrument of violence upon the cross denies its purity and superimposes on other truth which is contrary to the foundational truth of the cross.

THERE ARE MOTHERS WHO WANT THEIR CHILDREN TO BE BEST AND FIRST—NEITHER REALIZING NOR CARING WHAT THAT MEANS TO

THE MOTHERS AND CHILDREN WHO ARE LEAST AND LAST. THERE ARE MOTHERS WHO WHAT THEIR CHILDREN TO BE ALL THEY THEMSELVES COULD NEVER BE—NEITHER REALIZING NOR CARING THAT CHILDREN ARE NOT MADE IN OUR IMAGE BUT IN THE IMAGE OF GOD. **Elizabeth McAliser**

I RAISE UP MY VOICE TO SAY: DO NOT WORSHIP YOUR WEALTH! **Archbishop Oscar Romero**

[THE OTHER COUNTRIES] WILL HAVE TO SELL MORE AND BUY MORE. Prime Minister **Jean Chrétien**, referring to the formula for keeping "Free Trade" alive

SHOPPING IS GOOD. Recently publicity mantra of **The Bay**, Canadian retail giant

Q. You were not present, I don't believe, on April 2nd, 1999, is that correct?

A. No, I was not.

Q. But you've heard the evidence in the courtroom so far as to what happened on that occasion?

A. Yes, I've heard the evidence this morning.

Q. And do you know the defendants before the Court?

A. Yes. I have not known any of the defendants for a terribly long time. I have known Don Heap for, approximately, two years and the others for less than that time.

Q. Now, briefly, what is your view, as an Anglican priest, of the sword on the cross?

A. My view has shifted appreciably during the time I have worked at All Saints. I think that previously the sword, for me, was largely an abstract symbol and, therefore, did not command much attention. But working in the inner city, as I do, in a conflicted neighbourhood, as I do, the reality of violence at all levels has become much more real for me, and I have found myself increasingly made aware of scripture stories such as this: when Jesus was in the garden on the evening of his arrest, when he was confronted by soldiers, he neither fought them nor did he flee.

Instead he stood in active testimony to the truth that he carried. That is reality that has become more real for me. It is a reality which precludes violence, for violence is a diminishment of other human beings and the call for truth living that God places upon each one of us.

> WAR NOW SEEMS TO ME LIKE THE INFANTILE SICKNESS OF A HUMANITY WHICH HAS NOT YET UNDERSTOOD THAT DESTRUCTION DOES NOT RESOLVE PROBLEMS AND THAT IT DEGRADES HUMANS. **Général Jacques de Bollardiére**

Q. All right. In your parish you deal with persons who have very little means, in general? Isn't that fair to say?

A. For the most part, yes.

Q. And do you see any connection between military operations and that situation?

A. At any number of levels, although I would have to speak without great precision. Of course there is the directing of economic resources within any community and the economic resources do not tend to be directed as fully as they should be to the community of where I find myself working. There is also the spirit of the heart and the working of the mind which, when focusing upon the need to defend one's self, either dismisses or becomes indifferent to others who potentially cause a threat to our way of being. And I find that many people who are without means in our community are either left ignored or turned against because of the threat they presume upon others.

> IT'S SO MUCH HARDER TO FIGHT FOR YOUR LIBERTY IN A NONVIOLENT WAY THAN IT IS WITH A GUN. PEOPLE VERY CLOSE TO ME HAVE BEEN KILLED NOW, AND YET I STILL THINK THAT. PEOPLE IN OUR POSITIONS REALLY HAVE TO DIE UNTO OURSELVES AND OUR WEALTH TO GAIL THE SPIRITUALITY OF THE POOR AND OPPRESSED. **Jean Donovan**, former successful U.S. business woman who was murdered by the military for her persistent work with the poor in El Salvador

THE COURT: Could we bring this back to the case at the bar?
MR. ROSENTHAL:

Q. Yes, thank you. Now, you were present in court when His Honour was asking me to clarify the relationship between the theological aspects, one might say, of the action, and the law. But without speaking as a lawyer, can you shed any light on any of those issues as to three Christian persons doing this kind of action that was described on this occasion?

A. The cross is a central symbol of Christianity. It is above all a symbol of redemptive love. That kind of love affords no opportunity for violence. The imposition of an instrument of violence upon the cross denies its purity and superimposes another truth which is contrary to the foundational truth of the cross.

> THE MYTH OF REDEMPTIVE VIOLENCE ENSHRINES THE BELIEF THAT VIOLENCE SAVES, THAT WAR BRINGS PEACE, THAT MIGHT MAKES RIGHT. IT, AND NOT JUDAISM OR CHRISTIANITY OR ISLAM, IS THE DOMINANT RELIGION OF OUR SOCIETY TODAY. **Walter Wink**, U.S. biblical scholar
>
> MY MAJOR PART IN LIVING OUT THE MYTH OF "PAX AMERICANA" WAS TO SPEND A FEW YEARS IN THE U.S. AIR FORCE FOLLOWING GRADUATION FROM R.O.T.C. AT LOYOLA UNIVERSITY. AS I REFLECT ON THOSE YEARS IT MAKES ME CONSCIOUS OF HOW MUCH I HAD BOUGHT INTO THAT MYTH.
>
> **Louis Vitale**, Franciscan friar, active in nonviolent resistance to U.S. militarism

Q. Thank you very much for coming here today.

THE ACCUSED

DANIEL HEAP: AFFIRMED
EXAMINATION IN-CHIEF BY MR. ROSENTHAL:

Q. Good morning, Mr. Heap. Now, firstly what I'd like to ask you is why did you not swear on the Bible?

A. Well, I feel that it's tended to be used, not just in court but in many ways, as a kind of magic thing which degrades the actual meaning of it. In fact, as far back as the gospel, Jesus himself said, "Don't swear by the temple, by the heaven, by anything, just say yes or no," and I think that's common sense.

Q. I'd like to ask you a little bit about your background, sir. I understand that you were ordained as a priest? Is that correct, sir?

A. Yes, in 1952.

Q. 1952, and in what denomination is that, sir?

A. The Anglican Church, Diocese of Montreal.

Q. And are you still an Anglican priest?

A. Yes. I am now under the jurisdiction of the Bishop of Toronto.

Q. And you also had a political career, is that correct?

A. Well, in 1954 I asked my bishop for leave, not from the priesthood but from parish work, to work as a factory labourer. I thought the church—possibly especially the Anglican church—was so far from the manual working class and I wanted to follow the example of some of the clergy in Britain and Europe who were doing the same. So he gave me the leave and I came to Toronto. Then I opted, at the end of the leave, to stay in Toronto and that was accepted by the bishop and [by] several parishes in which I assisted as an honourary assistant, simply like a member of the parish but able to perform some functions that lay people don't do.

Q. And then did you have a political career as an elected official?

A. Then I became a candidate for an election first in 1968, federally, provincially in '71, and then in '72 I was elected to city council where I was re-elected until 1981, and then I was elected to Parliament where I served for 12 years.

> ACCORDING TO MY UNDERSTANDING OF ECONOMICS AND SOCIOLOGY, WAR IS THE INEVITABLE OUTCOME OF THE EXISTING SOCIAL ORGANIZATION WITH ITS UNDEMOCRATIC FORM OF GOVERNMENT AND COMPETITIVE SYSTEM OF INDUSTRY.

J.S. Woodsworth, a founder of the Cooperative Commonwealth of Canada (CCF) and a Member of Parliament.

Q. So was it 1972 to 1981 you were a city councillor?
A. Yes.
Q. And then from 1981 for 12 years you were a member of the federal Parliament of Canada?
A. Yes. I announced retirement before the 1993 election due to a physical condition.
Q. Physical condition?
A. Physical condition, running out of energy. Trinity/Spadina is a hard place to run.
Q. You had some energy on April 2nd, 1999, apparently, which we are here about.
A. Enough.
Q. Now we've heard some evidence, and we've admitted some facts, about an event that happened on April 2nd, 1999. Could you tell us, sir, first from your vantage point as a participant, about the discussions or communications that took place prior to that occasion and related to that occasion?
A. Well, I'll try to make it very short. When, in 1939, our family heard that Britain had declared war on Germany, I asked my parents if it's ever right for Christians to kill. The answer: usually not, but sometimes it's necessary and this is one of those times.

> WHEN THERE WAS PEACE,
> HE WAS FOR PEACE;
> WHEN THERE WAS WAR,
> HE WENT.
> **W. H. Auden**, from *The Unknown Citizen*

I wavered on that. I joined the army in '44, took the training, infantry and parachute and so on. I was not sent overseas because the war was winding down. They didn't send our class from Camp Charlotte. I went back to university and later was ordained. But I wavered still on the question of whether wars ought to be fought or, at least, whether they ought to be fought by Christians with weapons of death, and I didn't resolve it until 1991.

> HARK! IT IS THE SUMMONS OF
> THE BUGLE OF THE LORD
> HE CALLED THE MEN OF BRITAIN
> TO BECOME HIS LIVING SWORD...
> CALLED WITH NO UNCERTAIN CLAIM
> TO THE WOMEN OF GREAT BRITAIN...
> TOILING IN BRITANNIA'S KITCHENS
> THEY WILL FEED HER FIGHTING MEN.
> From ***Women in Wartime—***
> ***The Role of Women's Magazines 1939–1945***

I had been accepting, with some difficulties, the view that, while Jesus' advice is just great, there are some practical problems, and we might have to kill a few bad people to save a lot of good people, and that might be the real way of carrying out his commandment. After the Gulf War, I couldn't hold that any longer. We killed so many, even after the war, that I had to say, no. I finally answered the question I asked 52 years before. I think it's never right for Christians to kill under any circumstances—individually or collectively or internationally.

> ON WHAT AUTHORITY HAVE YOU WAGED SUCH
> DETESTABLE WARS AGAINST THESE PEOPLES
> WHO DWELT QUIETLY AND PEACEFULLY ON
> THEIR OWN LAND?
>
> **Antonio de Montesinos**, Dominican friar who risked his
> life denouncing his fellow Spaniards' violence against the
> indigenous people of "Hispaniola" (December, 1511)

Q. Your coming to that conclusion led to a sequence of events that brought you here today, is that correct?

A. Well, after a while, yes. When I became what I would call a pacifist—though sometimes only a passive sort of pacifism—I was fully convinced of the need for nonviolent active resistance. But I realized that habitually I haven't been a very non-violent person. I have a bad temper. I shout at people and so on. I quarrel and I've got to work on that.

THE PLOWSHARES EXPERIENCE STRENGTHENED MICHELE'S AND MY LOVE FOR EACH OTHER. I GAINED A DEEPER APPRECIATION FOR HER GIFTS AS WE WERE APART. APOLOGIES FOR PAST MISUNDERSTANDINGS AND CONFLICTS WERE MADE, AND WE CONTINUED THE PROCESS OF FORGIVING AND MAKING CHANGES AND TRYING TO COMMUNICATE BETTER. DISARMING A WEAPON AND DISARMING OURSELVES AND OUR EGOS CAN LEAD TO GROWTH IN STEADFAST LOVE.

Greg Boertge-Obed, member of Jonah House Community, from *Maternal Convictions*

So I didn't try to make any big decisions, particularly before I retired from Parliament. Since then, I've been working at it but I don't know when the Christian churches in Britain or Canada have condemned a war in which Britain and Canada won. That doesn't sound to me like a fair judgment, and I think it's got to be challenged.

I'VE LOOKED DOWN TOO MANY RIFLE BARRELS IN MY TIME TO BE SCARED THAT WAY. THIS THING'S IN OUR BLOOD FOR 400 YEARS AND YOU CAN'T TAKE IT AWAY FROM US LIKE YOU'D CRACK A PIECE OF KINDLING OVER YOUR KNEE. I WAS BEFORE A FIRING SQUAD TWICE. WE BELIEVE IN THIS. IT'S DEEP IN OUR BLOOD.

Jacob H. Janzen, Mennonite from Waterloo, refusing to cooperate with Canada's involvement in World War II and responding to Major General L. R. La Fleche's threat, "What'll you do if we shoot you?"

I HAVE BOYS OF MY OWN AND I HOPE THEY ARE NOT COWARDS, BUT IF ANY ONE OF THOSE BOYS, NOT FROM COWARDICE BUT REALLY THROUGH BELIEF, IS WILLING TO TAKE HIS STAND ON THIS

> MATTER [OF WAR] AND, IF NECESSARY, TO FACE A CONCENTRATION CAMP OR A FIRING SQUAD, I SHALL BE MORE PROUD OF THAT BOY THAN IF HE ENLISTED FOR THE WAR."
> **J. S. Woodsworth, Canada's "Prophet in Politics"**

There seems to be a very strong identification of Christianity with British patriotism. I don't agree with the edict of Henry VIII that said it is lawful for Christian men to wear weapons and serve in wars at the command of the magistrate. I think he was dealing with a desperate national emergency, but as a general future law for centuries, no, I don't think that stands.

> RECONCILIATION IS A UNIVERSAL PRINCIPLE, TO BE PRACTISED ON EVERY PLANE AND IN EVERY DEPARTMENT OF LIFE. IT IS TO BE PRACTISED TOWARD THE STRANGER AND TOWARD THE DIFFICULT NEIGHBOUR…IT IS THE FUNDAMENTAL PRINCIPLE BY WHICH WE SHOULD REGULATE OUR PUBLIC RELATIONS, OUR POLITICS, WHETHER DOMESTIC OR INTERNATIONAL, AND OUR COMMERCIAL AND PROFESSIONAL CONCERNS.
> **Richard Roberts**, sixth Moderator of the United Church of Canada

Q. Now, coming to your getting together with the two defendants to do something about the sword on the cross, could you tell us how you began your interest in that sword on the cross and what happened?

A. I was acquainted with Leonard Desroches, particularly, for a number of years in connection with peace activity around the Cruise Missile Conversion Project in the early eighties, when I was a Member of Parliament, and when we formed a group called Faith and Resistance.

> WE LIVE IN THE FLESH, OF COURSE, BUT THE MUSCLES THAT WE FIGHT WITH ARE NOT FLESH. OUR WAR IS NOT FOUGHT WITH WEAPONS OF

FLESH, YET THEY ARE STRONG ENOUGH, IN GOD'S CAUSE, TO DEMOLISH FORTRESSES.

Second letter to the community at Corinth (2 Cor. 10:3–4)

THE UNDERGROUND RAILROAD DIDN'T RUN ON STEAM

THE UNDERGROUND RAILROAD DIDN'T RUN ON COAL

THE POUNDING YOU HEARD WAS A PULSING BLOOD STREAM

WHAT MADE THE ROAD RUN WAS THE STRENGTH OF THE SOUL

Canadian folksong

And then the question came up that a monument in a very public place, on Bloor Street, seems to suggest that the cross goes with the sword and maybe even the cross goes in front of the sword. First the cross and then the sword, and for some people in the world that is the way it has seemed to be. And I think that's partly why the church is in trouble.

> THE CHURCHES LOST HEAVILY IN SPIRITUAL AUTHORITY BECAUSE OF THEIR GENERAL SURRENDER TO THE WAR SPIRIT IN 1941–18. *A Witness Against War*, 1939

Q. And then you and your fellow defendants formulated a plan with respect to that cross, did you?
A. Yes.
Q. And what was that plan?
A. Well, we felt that the sword must be taken off the cross, not at the end of another 17 centuries of debate in the church, because the situation is building up. We therefore asked St. Paul's Church to talk with us about it. They said, "We're getting close to Easter time, there isn't time." So

we began to distribute a leaflet outside while the service was ending and proposed that we would have a vigil there on the sidewalk. So then the priest in charge, the incumbent of the parish, invited us for a meeting and we met, as has been mentioned by the church warden, Mr. Forde.

In effect, as I think Mr. Forde made clear, the church representatives did not feel that the situation should be pursued. They said, "This is a matter for the higher authority and we have an obligation to maintain this monument that was put in our church yard." So we did another vigil and then we thought about it through the summer. I don't mean meeting every day. we all have our work.

Q. This was several years ago?

A. 1998

Q. 1998, yes.

A. Then we began to plan on St. Francis Day, the beginning of October, and then six vigils memorializing people like Archbishop Oscar Romero and so on, announcing that we were leading up to Good Friday and asking that the church—locally or regionally or whatever—at least make a start towards removing the sword and turning it into a ploughshare as a symbol of renunciation of war. There was no further communication, really, from the incumbent or other officers of the church. They observed us when we were doing the vigil there, along with other people, but there did not seem to be any concern for discussing the issue.

> ONE OF CHRIST'S ESSENTIAL COMMANDS WAS…BE BULLIED, BE OUTRAGED, BE KILLED; BUT DO NOT KILL. IT MAY BE CHIMERICAL AND AN IGNOMINIOUS PRINCIPLE, BUT THERE IT IS. IT CAN ONLY BE IGNORED, AND I THINK PULPIT PROFESSIONALS ARE IGNORING IT VERY SKILFULLY.
>
> **Wilfred Owen**, poet, in a 1917 letter to his mother

Then my bishop, the Bishop of Toronto, the Right Reverend Terence Finlay, wrote me a short letter asking me not to do it. I wrote back telling him why I thought I ought to do it. But there wasn't any discussion of the issue. There was a motion moved two years ago in the Tri-Annual

Synod meeting in Montreal calling for a discussion. It was referred to a committee which has referred it to a sub-committee, and we're still waiting to hear what direction that will give to parishes about discussing it.

> WE PLEDGE OURSELVES TO RENOUNCE WAR AND ALL PREPARATION TO WAGE WAR, AND TO WORK FOR THE CONSTRUCTION OF CHRISTIAN PEACE IN THE WORLD. Statement of the **Anglican Pacifist Fellowship**, England

Until yesterday when Bishop Finlay, himself, chaired a meeting hosted by the Reverend Jeannie Loughrey at All Saints Church for the purpose of discussing whether there could ever be a just war. Bishop Finlay referred to the events of the year before, that is, since we three were present amongst the 38 who were in the group.

> FAR FROM BEING THE VOCATION OF A MINORITY, PACIFISM WAS THE HALLMARK OF ORTHODOX CHRISTIANITY FOR OVER 200 YEARS SPECIFICALLY BECAUSE ONE COULD NOT TAKE UP ARMS AND KILL AN ENEMY AND STILL BE A CHRISTIAN.
>
> **Rev. Clive Barrett**, member of the Anglican Pacifist Fellowship

Q. Is it your conclusion that that meeting was possibly as a result of your actions that are before the Court?

A. The bishop seemed to suggest that. The point that we wanted to make is that the church has for too long traded with Caesar and the successors to Caesar, protection of church revenues and property in return for justification of every war that Caesar chooses to wage; and that the local symbol of that was the use of the state, that is, the police, to protect the property in the church yard, rather than engage actively in a discussion as to why it might be more proper to remove that sword.

> THE VIOLENCE WE PREACH IS NOT THE VIOLENCE OF THE SWORD, THE VIOLENCE OF HATRED. IT IS THE VIOLENCE OF LOVE. THE

> VIOLENCE THAT WILLS TO BEAT WEAPONS INTO SICKLES FOR WORK. **Archbishop Oscar Romero**

Q. Now did you feel that there was any urgency to your actions?

A. Yes. Particularly from '81 to '93, as a Member of Parliament it was my function for the caucus, as assigned to me, to review the Immigration Ministry. I was impressed with how many refugees were coming to Canada because of conditions that were directly or indirectly caused by the countries of Western Europe and North America who formerly had regular colonial empires and now have financial empires, and controlled them with whatever weapons they think necessary, including the threat of nuclear weapons. The church is too silent.

In fact—now I don't claim any connection here—but about, oh, two or three weeks after Good Friday when we were arrested for our attempt, the leaders of nine churches in Canada, including Anglican Archbishop Peers, asked Prime Minister Chretien to persuade NATO to hold a moratorium on the bombing of Kosovo so that negotiations could be reopened. The prime minister politely refused it.

> FOR ME THE TEACHINGS AND THE SPIRIT OF JESUS ARE ABSOLUTELY IRRECONCILABLE WITH THE ADVOCACY OF WAR.
> **J. S. Woodsworth**

THE COURT: I'm sorry. Again, I'd like to reel that in so that we can deal with the issue.

THE WITNESS: I'm sorry, Your Honour.

MR. ROSENTHAL:

Q. I believe Mr. Heap was trying to give the background, but perhaps you could more quickly go to the question of did you feel it was urgent for you to act in the way that you did on this occasion, April 2nd, 1999?

A. Yes. The killing of Iraqis has continued for ten years now, nine years then, mainly through the sanctions, and other wars fuelled by, or at least armed by, countries, including Canada—sometimes armed on both sides. And the churches are making no substantial objection to that. The churches sort of say, "Isn't it too bad," but they don't say "It's wrong!"

THAT SPIRITUALITY AND WORK [OF NONVIOLENCE] WITH PEOPLE'S CONSCIENCES HAD NEVER BEEN DONE. WE HAVE NO RIGHT TO HOPE TO HARVEST WHAT WE HAVE NOT SOWN.

Miguel d'Escoto, priest and former Minister of Foreign Affairs for Nicaragua, speaking of his failed attempts to have the Nicaraguan bishops risk nonviolent resistance to the brutal Somoza military dictatorship

Q. And did you think that your actions would have any effect on that, or could possibly have an effect on it?

A. I wasn't sure how much effect it could have, but I couldn't think of anything better to do for that purpose, to try and draw the attention of the church I belong to, the Anglican church, which happens to be the one that has put a sword in front of the cross. I'm not sure whether other churches have that or not, but we do in one parish.

Q. You were here for the discussion by several previous witnesses about whether the sword on the cross is blasphemous or somehow contradictory to the message of the cross. What is your view on that, sir?

A. I think it is a blasphemy. It's a total denial of what the cross is about. The cross is meant for life and the sword is meant for death.

Q. So given that belief, sir, how would you characterize your attempt to remove the sword?

A. I believed I was following the fundamental reaching and direction and commandment of God through the Christian Church and through Jesus.

Q. Now, on the occasion of April 2nd, 1999, when you attended, was it your intention to actually remove that sword, or what was your intention?

A. I didn't think that we would actually be able to finish the job, even though we had the mountain climber's straps to hold us on to the monument. But I thought we should make a start, and we might make a start at the bottom, maybe pry the point of the sword off as a sign of a beginning or a possible beginning.

Q. And if you had succeeded in beginning, if you had pried the bottom up a bit, in your view how would that affect this monument as a Christian symbol? Would it improve or detract from the monument to do that?

A. I thought that if we could begin taking the sword off, it would help to restore the cross to its true and life-giving meaning.

Q. Is there anything else that you'd like to say about what you did on that occasion or why you did it, sir?

A. No. I can't think of anything, no.

Q. Thank you very much, sir. There may be questions from other counsel.

CROSS EXAMINATION BY MR. MCCOMB:

Q. Reverend Heap, were you actually intending on pulling yourself up on that monument with straps? Would you have done that if you got there?

A. I'm not the mountaineer in our group. I wondered how we were going to hang onto it while we could do any work and Bob Holmes said, "Well, I've got my straps from mountain climbing. We'll just strap ourselves on."

Q. Thank you, sir.

CROSS EXAMINATION BY MR. CARRINGTON:

Q. Yes. Good afternoon, sir. Sir, when Mr. Rosenthal was asking you questions, you mentioned that your bishop wrote you a letter asking you not to proceed with the actions that you did undertake on April 2nd, 1999?

A. That's true, yes.

Q. Okay. And was one of the reasons that the bishop asked you not to proceed with the action was because the bishop suggested it was illegal?

A. I didn't bring the letter with me, so I don't remember for sure, but I think not. I think what he said was it would only sort of polarize the discussion rather than facilitating the understanding of each other. My feeling was that the discussion had been polarized for 18 centuries, 17 centuries.

Q. All right. Now, sir, what, if any, alternatives were discussed by you and Mr. Holmes and Mr. Desroches besides taking the action that you did on April 2nd, 1999?

A. Well, while we were carrying on our vigils, beginning on October 4th and then going a little more than once a month, six more vigils, we were trying to discuss it with anybody that we found wanted to discuss it. And we did write to the leaders of the six mainline churches in the area inviting them to comment, and inviting them to take some action in the matter. And then we announced that we would be going to hold a prayer vigil in front of each of those six offices, which we did, on the first two days of the week before Easter, Holy Week—except for the Anglican office, because Bishop Finlay had phoned me and invited us to actually meet with him on Monday night of Holy Week.

So we didn't propose a vigil in front of his office that day. At the other churches, we had some discussion with the people that were there and some of them were quite interested. But none took what we thought was a positive step. Nor did Bishop Finlay at that time.

Q. Did you consider having further discussions and perhaps bringing other parties into the discussions?

A. We didn't know how to bring other parties into the discussions since church authorities had not seemed much interested, particularly Anglican and, above all, Roman Catholic church authorities. In the case of the Anglican Church, I had some hope that a motion passed in our Tri-Annual General Synod the year before our action would be generating some discussion. It was intended to do that. It called for a discussion in the parishes.

It was referred to a small committee that has little staff and nothing came out. Nothing has come out yet. So we didn't think there was much chance of getting discussion going, although we were delighted when the priest at All Saints sponsored the meeting, which Bishop Finlay chaired, for a debate around this issue. It has opened it up, I think, wonderfully.

> WE CAN ONLY REGRET THAT WE ARE SO FAR BEHIND IN THE MATTER OF A GOOD CHRISTIAN THEORY AND POWERFUL PRACTICE OF NONVIOLENCE.
>
> Catholic Bishop **Dennis Hurley**, South Africa, during the resistance to apartheid
>
> IF THIS ENTERPRISE, THIS MOVEMENT OF THEIRS, IS OF HUMAN ORIGIN IT WILL BREAK UP OF ITS OWN ACCORD; BUT IF IT DOES IN

> FACT COME FROM GOD YOU WILL NOT ONLY BE UNABLE TO DESTROY THEM, BUT YOU MIGHT FIND YOURSELVES FIGHTING AGAINST GOD.
>
> **Gamaliel**, the Pharisee, advising the Sanhedrin on how to treat the apostles who refused to stop proclaiming Christ's message of radical, unarmed justice and mercy (Acts 5:38–39)

Q. Did you not think of going back to that committee that was established to deal with the issue?

A. I phoned to find out what they were doing. I was told that the chairman was in another dioceses and I could phone him if I wished and so on. But I also understood that they were discussing, you might say, not the content but the procedure. So I thought, if we're only at the procedural stage there is nothing going to happen until shortly before the next Tri-Annual Synod, and then they'll present a report to Synod. What it would say, I don't know.

Q. When was the next Tri-Annual Synod?

A. It will be in the year 2000.

Q. All right. And did you consider waiting until the next Tri-Annual Synod?

A. No, we did not.

Q. Why not?

A. We thought that there was not really much reason to wait for it when it didn't seem urgent. It seemed urgent to us with the Iraq War really continuing through the sanction. It didn't seem that there was a sense of urgency in the churches.

> A TRUE REVOLUTION OF VALUES WILL SOON LOOK UNEASILY ON THE GLARING CONTRAST OF POVERTY AND WEALTH. WITH RIGHTEOUS INDIGNATION, IT WILL LOOK ACROSS THE SEAS AND SEE INDIVIDUAL CAPITALISTS OF THE WEST INVESTING HUGE SUMS OF MONEY IN ASIA, AFRICA, AND SOUTH AMERICA, ONLY TO TAKE THE PROFITS OUT WITH NO CONCERN FOR THE SOCIAL BETTERMENT OF THE COUNTRIES AND SAY: "THIS IS NOT JUST." A TRUE REVOLUTION

OF VALUES WILL LAY HANDS ON THE WORLD ORDER AND SAY OF WAR: "THIS WAY OF SETTLING DIFFERENCES IS NOT JUST." THIS BUSINESS OF BURNING HUMAN BEINGS WITH NAPALM, OF FILLING OUR NATION'S HOMES WITH ORPHANS AND WIDOWS, OF INJECTING POISONOUS DRUGS OF HATE INTO THE VEINS OF PEOPLES NORMALLY HUMANE, OF SENDING MEN HOME FROM DARK AND BLOODY BATTLEFIELDS PHYSICALLY HANDICAPPED AND PSYCHOLOGICALLY DERANGED CANNOT BE RECONCILED WITH WISDOM, JUSTICE, AND LOVE.

Martin Luther King Jr., *Conscience and the Vietnam War*. Almost the same number of U.S. soldiers committed suicide as were otherwise killed in the war in Vietnam: approximately 50,000

THE COURT: These discussions that you've been talking about since we reconvened, were these discussions about war or opposition to war in general terms, or were these discussions about what you were planning to do on the 2nd of April?
THE WITNESS: Well, the discussions that were proposed the year before at the General Synod were on war generally.
THE COURT: Right.
THE WITNESS: And, you know, war or not war.
THE COURT: Right.
THE WITNESS: The General Synod wasn't talking about our event
THE COURT: Yes, that's what I thought.
THE WITNESS: Yeah. But what we had told Bishop Finlay when he convened this meeting—which I thought was a very useful meeting, even though it didn't go to the point of resolving the matter—when Bishop Finlay said, "Well, what do you expect of the regional leaders?" We said, "Well, if one of the regional leaders of the churches, such as he, would say, "I will take this up and do what I can to persuade my church to look at doing that," we told him that would make us seriously reconsider our plans. But he made no such statement that night with us. It was a very friendly engagement, but it didn't go to that point.

THE COURT: But the discussion about the monument, that was part of the discussion?

THE WITNESS: Oh, that was why he called us to his office, yes.

THE COURT: That's why he called you?

THE WITNESS: It was all about that. But he said to me at one point, "Well, have you phoned Church House… (they're our national headquarters) "to find out what is happening pursuant to that motion?" I said, "Yes. I phoned several times and there is no definite news. I'm just told there is a sub-committee of a committee that's meeting." And he didn't pursue that challenge further.

MR CARRINGTON:

Q. But you could have done more to find out what exactly the committee was proposing, though.

A. Theoretically…

Q. Sorry. You could have done more to find out exactly what the committee was proposing to do, couldn't you?

A. Theoretically, we could have done more. Whether we would have learned more, I wasn't sure, and what we would have learned might have been so rudimentary or elementary as to be not significant. There are all kinds of conscious or unconscious delaying tactics, when people don't want to talk about something, [when] they have other things that seem much more important to do. The church seemed not to want to talk about the question of war.

Q. All right. And the reason that this action was undertaken on April 2nd, 1999, Good Friday, was because of the symbolic importance of that particular day, correct?

A. Yes.

Q. For example, it could have been done on an earlier date but that was deemed the most symbolically important date, correct?

A. Yes. Since the cross is, you might say, associated with Good Friday, or Good Friday with the cross.

Q. Okay. And do you agree, sir, that the police did warn you on April 2nd, 1999, before you climbed the fence to get on to the church property, that you would be arrested if you did so?

A. Yes. They did not suggest we would be charged with mischief. That happened after we got to the police station.

Q. Is it your evidence that they suggested you would be charged with trespass?

A. Trespass, yes.

Q. Okay. They made it clear to you that you would be arrested for breaking the law?

A. Well, I understand there is a law of trespass.

Q. All right.

A. I think it is a law that normally I uphold, actively or passively, but I don't think it is of sufficient weight to be reason for not taking action to try to end the kind of killing that has been going on in places like Iraq.

> CIVIL DISOBEDIENCE IS THE INHERENT RIGHT OF A CITIZEN [WHO] DARE NOT GIVE IT UP WITHOUT CEASING TO BE HUMAN. **Gandhi**

Q. Thank you.

THE COURT: Thank you, sir.

MR. ROSENTHAL: No re-examination. Thank you.

LEONARD DESROCHES: AFFIRMED
EXAMINATION IN-CHIEF BY MR. MCCOMB:

Q. Mr. Desroches, I'll ask you to speak up here so everybody can hear you. How old are you, sir?

A. I'm 52.

Q. I understand you grew up in Penetanguishene?

A. I did.

Q. And you attended seminaries in both Canada and the United States?

A. That's correct.

Q. You trained for the priesthood?

A. Yes.

Q. To keep yourself in food and a roof over your head, I understand you do drywalling?

A. That's my wage-earning trade, yes.

> AFTER THE HUNGER STRIKE, I WAS TOTALLY CONVINCED THAT THIS WAS THE WAY; THAT NONVIOLENCE WAS NOT JUST A TACTIC BUT THAT IT WAS THE CORE OF OUR WORK.

Joao Breno, Brazilian labour leader, during the famous *Perus* strike

Q. Thank you. You've heard Mr. Heap give evidence just now. You heard that?

A. Yes, I did.

Q. Anything you particularly wish to comment or disagree with about what he said?

A. No. I have no comments on Mr. Heap, sir.

Q. His recollection of the chronology of events is similar to yours?

A. Yes, it is.

Q. All right.

A. Well, except for the Court's record, Reverend Holmes and Reverend Heap heard the police say that we were going to be arrested for trespass. I happen to not have heard that...

Q. Okay. I believe, sir, if I understood the Court correctly here, that your motive in doing what you did is understood and accepted. But can I ask you what you intended to achieve by your actions prior to going to the church that day?

A. What we intended to achieve was to address a very destructive symbol, a symbol that profoundly and dangerously confuses the Christian community with the imposition of the sword on the cross. This gives a clear message that the cross itself is not a force. [The cross] may be a good thing. It may be a very good thing. It may be socially sanctioned but when we have serious problems, like in Iraq, when we have enemies, when we are threatened and so forth, we need the force of the sword. And that's why it's imposed. In that sense it could not be a more accurate representation of the confusion—it ranges from confusion to hypocrisy—in the case of the church.

The symbol of the sword on the cross dangerously perpetuates warfare in the world. I admit that the sword is a force. I have tremendous respect—I say this sincerely—for people in the armed forces who believe in this force. I believe it is a force [as] for example in its organized form as armies.

I also happen to believe there is another force in the world that's even stronger. That is the force of love, of truth-saying. This is literally a force. The cross of itself represents that force and does not need the sword to be a force. The heart of this is the mystery, the live-giving mystery of love of enemy. I acknowledge that that's a tremendously difficult thing. I do not acknowledge that it's impossible [to love your enemy]—at least not with the grace of God.

> AS MUCH AS CANADIANS WOULD LIKE TO IGNORE THE FACT, THE ROLE OF A SOLDIER IS TO KILL AS EFFICIENTLY AS POSSIBLY WITH THE RESOURCES AVAILABLE ONCE HE IS ORDERED TO DO SO BY HIS GOVERNMENT. THERE ARE MANY SIDELINES TO HIS PROFESSION THAT MAKE US ALL FEEL WARM AND FUZZY. BUT THEY ARE SUBORDINATE TO ONE OVERRIDING RESPONSIBILITY, AND THAT IS TO KILL ON DEMAND. **General Lewis Mackenzie**, (Canada) May 2000

> THIS STRATEGY IS ACCESSIBLY TO THE MASSES. AT ITS WORST, THIS STRUGGLE WITHOUT ARMS AND WITHOUT HATRED WOULD NOT PROVOKE THE SAME MASSACRES AS VIOLENCE, WOULD NOT ACCUMULATE THE SAME RUINS, WOULD NOT LOWER THE LEVEL OF CIVILIZATION. AS AN OFFICER, I HAVE CONSTANTLY ASKED YOUNG MEN TO ACCEPT TO BE KILLED. AND THEY ACCEPTED, OFTEN WITHOUT UNDERSTANDING, SIMPLY BECAUSE THEY WERE TRAINED FOR THAT. WHY WOULD NOT YOUNG PEOPLE TODAY ACCEPT TO SACRIFICE THEMSELVES FOR SOMETHING THAT THEY UNDERSTAND AND BELIEVE IN? **Général Jacques de Bollardiére**

> NOW I SHOULD LIKE TO CHALLENGE THE IMPLICATION THAT, IN ORDER THAT WE MAY BECOME A SELF-SUFFICIENT NATION, IT IS NECESSARY FOR US TO MAINTAIN A MILITIA FORCE. NOW IS THE TIME WHEN WE SHOULD DECIDE WHETHER OR NOT AN ARMED FORCE MEANS OR MAKES FOR PEACE. I RECOGNIZE

THAT THE POLICY WHICH I HAVE ADVOCATED WOULD INVOLVE RISKS, BUT THE PRESENT POLICY INVOLVES NOT ONLY RISKS BUT ALMOST CERTAIN FAILURE. WHY NOT TAKE THOSE RISKS WHICH ARE INCIDENT TO THE DEVELOPMENT OF THE NEW MEANS OF PROTECTING OUR NATIONS?
J. S. Woodsworth

IN THE LAST FEW YEARS, TWO COUNTRIES IN LATIN AMERICA HAVE TAKEN HISTORIC STEPS TOWARD ENDING ONCE AND FOR ALL THE VICIOUS CYCLE OF POVERTY AND MILITARISM. FOLLOWING THE RESTORATION OF DEMOCRACY TO PANAMA IN 1989 AND TO HAITI IN 1994, I HELPED PERSUADE BOTH COUNTRIES TO CONSTITUTIONALLY ABOLISH THEIR NATIONAL ARMIES, AS COSTA RICA ITSELF DID IN 1949. **Oscar Arias**, Nobel Peace laureate and former president of Costa Rica

Q. …physically what were you going to ultimately do to this cross?
A. We had been challenged along the way to recognize that this cross represented something very important to the relatives of those who had died. For me war, the sword, the institution of war is the sending of the young to die and to kill for us. If we do that we have a moral responsibility to have a war memorial. We did not disagree.

I WOULD JUST LIKE MY LIFE BACK. BEFORE I WENT TO THE GULF I WAS HEALTHY, HAD NO PAIN, TOOK NO PILLS AND WAS ABLE TO SLEEP. **Eldon Berghamer**, Canadian Gulf War veteran (Toronto Star, Feb. 19, 2000); as many as 100,000 of the 700,000 soldiers who served in the Gulf War complain of symptoms, which many attribute to exposure to chemicals

We publicly made it clear that far from wanting to damage that war memorial, we had utter respect for it. We were uniquely addressing the sword in the middle of the cross. We were pleading and challenging the leaders to respectfully, and as workers to skilfully, take the sword off and transform it into a ploughshare according to the Prophet Isaiah, "They shall beat their swords into ploughshares." In doing so we were not suggesting disrespect in relationship to the war memorial—far from it.

Q. Sir, I'm showing you a flyer which hasn't made it into evidence yet. Do you recognize this piece of paper that I'm showing you?

> We intended to address a very destructive symbol: the position of the sword on the cross is a very clear message that the cross of itself is not a force; that when we have enemies, we need the force of the sword
>
> The symbol of the sword on the cross perpetuates warfare.
>
> Unless we come to terms as a church with our role in warfare nothing will change and wars will be perpetuated.
>
> We felt it was a moral imperative for the church to do something beyond words, beyond statements, about the renunciation of the institution of war.

Yes, I do.
Q. What is this piece of paper?
A. It's one of the many leaflets that we prepared to help people at the church—out of respect because it happened to be on their property—and for the public walking by…
Q. Did you author or participate in authoring this document?
A. I did.

Q. There is a line here I want to ask you about. "We fully respect the need for a memorial for the war dead." Was that, is that your position today?

A. It is.

Q. And that was your position at the time you...

A. Yes.

Q. ...performed your actions? Can I ask that this be made an exhibit, Your Honour?

THE COURT: Yes.

MR. MCCOMB: Thank you.

CLERK OF THE COURT: Exhibit number 8.

EXHIBIT NUMBER 8: Leaflet

Produced and Marked.

MR. MCCOMB:

Q. We heard from the first witness in this matter that you attempted to raise this issue and have it discussed and aired within, I take it, the Congregation of St. Paul's Anglican Church, was that the idea?

A. Initially.

Q. Right, yes, initially.

A. That was simply out of respect for the fact that it was on their property. We would have wished it was on maybe the Canadian Council of Churches' property in the sense of it representing all the denominations...

Q. Was it their response that, "You're talking to the wrong people, you've got to take it higher up"?

A. I think it was eventually. Initially we were simply two groups of people who were trying to understand each other. "What are you doing on our property? Why are you picking on us?" We understood that would be a legitimate impression and so we thought, yes, let's meet as two groups and...

Q. Did you, if I may lead you, to cut to the chase here, did you feel stonewalled...

A. M'hmm, m'hmm.

Q. What was your reaction to that position?

A. I was hoping for another response but I was not surprised because, like Reverend Heap, I do understand my own church history enough to know what we've been doing this for at least 17 centuries. What I'm referring to is the polite discussion while the urgency of starvation, child soldiers, depleted uranium continues. As Bishop Gumbleton says, we have actually come to a place of absolute warfare. So I did not go with the illusion that we would necessarily get very far in the conversation, but I sincerely went with the hope for that conversation. I can say that quite honestly.

Q. Did you think that you were breaking the law by attempting to remove this sword?

A. Not at all. I honestly did accept the possibility of being arrested, but as Bishop Gumbleton explained this morning, I think I would not only have a right to destroy the crematoriums of the Nazis—a legally elected government by the way—I think I would have a tremendous moral responsibility. During the Iraq war, for about two weekends, I didn't know what to do except to pray. I accidentally walked by [the cross & sword war memorial] because I don't live far from there. My body completely surprised me and this gushing of water came out when I saw the sword and the cross. I was surprised by this. I don't cry for nothing. I thought about it and realized that the decades that I've been working against the institution of war have always been directed at either governments or corporations.

It began to dawn on me, with the kind of intensity that I hadn't yet experienced, that until I addressed my own faith community, in which I'm an active member (not only the Catholic Church but the wider Christian Church) that the war-making will never stop.

> [WE] MUST BE ABLE TO READ AGAIN THE GOSPELS AND TO EMBRACE THE ATTITUDE OF THE FIRST CHRISTIANS WHO REJECTED WAR, EVEN IF THEIR LIVES WERE ENDANGERED.
> **Bishop Adolphe Proulx**

Q. I want to distinguish between the feeling that you have had about the moral obligation, you have no legal training, I take it?

A. No, I don't.

Q. Nevertheless, as apart from your moral dictates, did you have an understanding, at whatever level, did you think that you were breaking the law?

A. Not in the least. I want to be clear: I did know of the very real possibility of being arrested. Yet I did feel that the greater wisdom, the more expansive understanding of the law, is that you cannot hold trespassing (or whatever we might have been charged with) to be greater than reacting to what you think is an urgent need. I have deep respect for laws. Some of them I don't think are that useful, but even those I follow diligently. But it's evident in history that laws are consistently, constantly changing.

We used to have laws that protected apartheid. They have changed. We have laws now that protect the churches who have memorials that give a destructive impression and direction to the Christian community—namely, that you can both do war and love your enemy. An even more serious message is that the cross is not a power, that it needs the sword in order to be effective.

> IN A PRISON, NO CHAINS, NOT EVEN A SENTENCE OF DEATH CAN ROB A MAN OF THE FAITH AND HIS OWN FREE WILL. GOD GIVES SO MUCH STRENGTH, A STRENGTH FAR STRONGER THAN ALL THE MIGHT OF THE WORLD. THE POWER OF GOD CANNOT BE OVERCOME.
>
> **Franz Yagerstatter**, in a letter to his wife from a Nazi cell where he was imprisoned for refusing to join the army

Q. You have had a previous experience with a trespassing charge in a totally different context, right?

A. Yes.

Q. Did anything as a result of that experience colour your views of your legal situation here?

A. Very much so. Some of us were asked to help the Innu (who live in what we white European folks call Labrador) in their tremendous struggle against foreigners doing low-level war games over their territory—destroying their source of food, destroying their children, tremendous violations and physical destruction of their way of life. We'd been asked to do a very small thing which was to participate in an international symbolic gesture of solidarity. So we occupied a consulate. We were arrested for trespass.

In the course of the trial, the judge agreed with us in the end that the defence of necessity applied here. He agreed that it was urgent. And we were acquitted on that defence.

> I AM PREPARED TO HOLD THAT THE DEFENDANTS BROKE THE LETTER OF THE LAW BY NON-COMPLIANCE TO PREVENT A GREATER EVIL, THAT IS, TO PREVENT THE DESTRUCTION OF THE INNU PEOPLE AND THEIR BASIC HUMAN RIGHTS. Justice of the Peace **Robert Phillips**, as he dismissed the charges against nine Innu supporters who were charged with trespassing during an occupation of the Dutch consulate in Toronto, April 10, 1996

I have a personal letter from Judge Ulf Panzer who did what I did. Judge Ulf Panzer is a West German judge who, along with I think it's 15 other judges, did what we had done over and over in front of Litton Systems—namely blockade a U.S. nuclear weapons base ([in his case] in West Germany.) He sent me his statement as he appeared before his brother judge to explain how he was not only morally bound to do this, but [how] legally this [action] was the greater meaning of the law.

Q. And perhaps finally, sir, did you think at the time that you were doing this, these acts, that there was any urgency to these things?

A. Well, as I said, I was surprised by my reaction during the Gulf War to that symbol. It could seem like an innocent symbol that hardly anybody notices. But I felt a tremendous urgency to address my own faith community regarding the ways that we perpetuate right now the starvation of Iraqis—or wherever the present war is. You can barely keep up with the wars today!

Q. And as pertains to the charge that's before this court...

A. M'hmm.

Q. I know you hold wide, well thought out series of positions on things. Can I ask you if I've missed anything? Is there anything you want to particularly say in respect of this offence that's before the Court?

A. I feel an urgency for the young people who somehow almost miraculously still feel connected to the church. Unless we come to terms as a church with our role in warfare, nothing will change and wars will be perpetuated.

> CAN THE KILLERS OF TODAY BE THE LEADERS OF TOMORROW? MUST WE DESTROY IN ORDER TO BUILD? I REFUSE TO BELIEVE THAT IT IS NECESSARY FOR A NATION TO BUILD ITS FOUNDATIONS ON THE BONES OF ITS YOUNG. **Benigno Aquino**, explaining his decision to return to the Philippines to confront the military dictatorship with nonviolent resistance. He was shot as he came off a plane which had just landed in the Philippines

Q. Thank you. Just stay there.
THE COURT: Just a second here. Do you wish to cross-examine?
MR. SALVATERRA: No question.
THE COURT: Okay, fine.
MR. ROSENTHAL: I have a couple of questions, sir.
THE COURT: Okay.

CROSS EXAMINATION BY MR. ROSENTHAL:

Q. Mr. Desroches, you were in court this morning when there was a discussion as to whether the sword and the cross is actually blasphemous?
A. Yes, I was.
Q. What is your view of that, sir?
A. The cross is an expression of God's power. It is a symbol of God's power. There are two forces. There is the force [of violence], which, in its organized form [is] the army. The end goal is victory over. Many people believe in that. I respect that. I fundamentally disagree.

> WHETHER ASPIRING CHAMPIONS OF RELIGION ARE MOTIVATED BY PRIVATE EGO OR BY THAT COLLECTIVE MANIFESTATION OF EGO KNOWN AS EMPIRE, THE RESULTS ARE LIKELY TO BE THE SAME. POWER IS NOT A MAGIC TROPHY TO BE FOUGHT FOR, BUT AN INFINITE SPIRITUAL RESOURCE. POWER BECOMES OBSCURED WHEN

WORLDLY DOMINANCE IS ASCENDANT. IT COMES TO THE FORE WHEN DOMINANCE IS REJECTED.
Rabia Terri Harris, *Muslim Peace Fellowship* (U.S.A.)

EACH HUMAN ENCOUNTER CAN MOVE US CLOSER TO THE TRUTH. WE ARE DEPENDENT ON EACH OTHER FOR ARRIVING AT THE TRUTH WHICH OUR SOURCES CONTAIN. WE ARE, IN FACT, EACH OTHER'S MOST INDISPENSABLE RESOURCE.
Rabbi Jeremy Milgrom, *Clergy for Peace,* and *Rabbis for Human Rights*, Israel

TOMORROW'S PEACE MUST BE DECIDED TODAY, WITH YESTERDAY'S ENEMY. **Udi Levy**, Israel peace activist

IF WE COULD READ THE SECRET HISTORY OF OUR ENEMIES, WE SHOULD FIND IN EACH LIFE SORROW AND SUFFERING ENOUGH TO DISARM ALL HOSTILITY. **Longfellow**

There is another force whose end goal is reconciliation—possibly the most difficult thing on earth. I believe in that force, along with Martin Luther King, along with the Village of Le Chambon in the south of France where roughly 5,000 Christians risked their lives to save approximately 5,000 Jews under the nose of the Nazis in occupied France. They refused to hate the Nazis because most Nazis were ordinary people, like most soldiers are; but they refused to accept the desolation of the Jews and they refused to not take the risks. They believed in this force [of nonviolence]. And they understood very clearly the risks they were taking, which were as great as the risks of any armed revolution.

ALL WHO AFFIRM THE USE OF VIOLENCE ADMIT IT IS ONLY A MEANS TO ACHIEVE JUSTICE AND PEACE. BUT PEACE AND JUSTICE ARE NONVIOLENCE…THE FINAL END OF HISTORY. THOSE WHO ABANDON NONVIOLENCE HAVE NO

> SENSE OF HISTORY. RATHER THEY ARE BYPASSING HISTORY, FREEZING HISTORY, BETRAYING HISTORY. **André Trocmé**, pastor of the Nazi-occupied French village of Le Chambon

Q. Now, on the occasion of April 2nd, 1999, did you intend to remove the sword from the cross entirely, or what was your intention?

A. We had talked about it and we had prayed about it. The intention actually was to [merely] begin to do it, because we thought that was more important. We really had over and over pleaded and challenged the church leaders to do it themselves. We said we would step aside. I would have been very happy if a church leader had come to do it because we felt it was a moral imperative for the church to do something beyond words, beyond statements, about the renunciation of the institution of war. And so we wanted to simply begin to do it in order that it could be finished by the church.

> GENERALLY WHAT HAPPENS IS THAT PEOPLE WILL STUDY NONVIOLENCE, READ BOOKS, GO TO SEMINARS WHERE THEY DISCUSS NONVIOLENCE AND ATTEND ENDLESS MEETINGS. NONVIOLENCE BECOMES JUST AN IDEOLOGY. THE IDEOLOGY BECOMES A LUXURY, NOT A WAY OF LIFE.
> **Cesar Chavez**

Q. So what would the beginning have consisted of if you hadn't been charged?

A. Barely... anything, anything symbolic, if we could begin to bend the sword—anything.

Q. And you would have stopped at that point?

A. Definitely.

Q. And then if you would have left the monument in that state, in your view, how would it compare to the present state from the viewpoint of...

A. Well I can only repeat what Ms. Janet Somerville and the bishop said. Namely, that as a Christian symbol, as a spiritual and religious symbol, it would free up the cross to speak for what it is. It would free it up from the desecration and the real blasphemy that is now imposed on it.

Q. Thank you very much, sir. Thank you, Your Honour.

CROSS EXAMINATION BY MR. CARRINGTON:

Q. Sir, I'm just going to show you what's been marked as Exhibit 6 in this proceeding. It's a number of pages, one of which is attached to the "Cross & Sword Newsletter," of December 1998.

A. M'hmm.

Q. It's the last page of the exhibit. It's double-sided so the second last page of the exhibit.

A. That's the leaflet, yeah.

Q. Just above the signatures the paragraph reads, "If you feel called to participate in the risk of arrest on Good Friday, there are two important conditions: (1) that you be actively engaged in one of the mainline churches; (2) that you fully accept the decision that the risk of arrest is part of the Good Friday action: that we will actually aim to physically take the sword off the cross on Good Friday." That's how it reads, correct?

A. That's correct.

Q. All right. Was that the initial intention of yourself and your colleagues?

A. Well, to be honest, we had considered whether that was the wisest thing or not, but we came to a very clear conclusion that, rather than attempt to take off the whole sword, we should actually [only] begin to do it.

Q. Okay. So there was a conscious decision to change the nature of your demonstration to only begin to take it off?

A. Yes.

Q. All right. And you acknowledge, sir, that you were likely to be arrested for breaking the law of trespass by entering on to the church's property. You acknowledge that that was likely to happen?

A. I acknowledge that that was possible. I wouldn't use the word likely because…

Q. Okay. And you acknowledge that you're aware of the existence of the law of trespass at the time?

A. Yes.

Q. Now you referred to something about a certain law having a greater meaning. What law are you talking about?

A. I referred to?

Q. You used words to the effect that there was a greater meaning, that a certain law had a greater meaning. What law?

A. Well, I was simply referring to, for example, the defence of necessity, where if I break the door down at your house and I have no reason to, that's just simply wrong and against the law. If [however] I did it to save your two children, the defence of necessity instructs the system that we should understand that there was a greater action taken. There was something broken, private property was broken, but it was in order to save a human life. I would agree with the bishop that property does not have rights. People have rights and we should use property in a proper way. There is property that's used to poison people. There is depleted uranium, that's property. I don't believe it even has a right to exist.

> I HOPE THE U.S. AND U.K. GOVERNMENTS FINALLY REALIZE THAT BY CONTINUING TO USE THIS AMMUNITION [DEPLETED URANIUM] THEY ARE POISONING THEIR OWN SOLDIERS.

> U.S. Army Col. **Dr. Asaf Durakovic**, former head of Nuclear Medicine at the U.S. Army's Veterans' Affairs facility in Delaware. Durakovic left the U.S. because he was told his life would be in danger if he continued his research on the effects of Depleted Uranium (D.U.). D.U. is a toxic nuclear waste material used to coat missiles and bullets; because of its great density it can penetrate tanks and armoured vehicles and burn on impact. It remains radioactive for 4,500 years.

> MY DAUGHTER LIVES IN BULGARIA. SHE LOST HER BABY IN PREGNANCY AT FOUR MONTHS, IN SEPTEMBER 1999. HER DOCTORS, INCLUDING A GYNECOLOGIST, TOLD HER THAT THEY HAD EXPERIENCED SEVERAL MISCARRIAGES AROUND THIS TIME DUE TO THE HEAVY D.U. BOMBING OF BELGRADE, CLOSE TO THE BULGARIAN BORDER.

Annette Oudejans, from St. Clements, Ontario, in a letter to the author, November, 2000

Q. So all you're talking about is really some higher moral authority as opposed to any.

A. No, I'm not—not at all. Until I began this maybe 20 years ago, with Peter Rosenthal and others, I did not understand the law. But I began to understand that there were things in the legal system that really could encompass a greater moral [reality] [that] you could come to a position, even within the system, of addressing a moral imperative which could be contained even within the legal system.

ROBERT HOLMES: SWORN
EXAMINATION IN-CHIEF BY MR. SALVATERRA:

Q. It's Reverend Holmes, is it not?
A. Yes, it is.
Q. Could you tell us a bit about your background?
A. I'm a Catholic priest. I belong to a religious community called the Congregation of St. Basil. I have taught high school for 30 years. I was a principal for six. I am working in formation in my community right now. I am working with the young members who are studying theology, preparing for priesthood.

> MILITARY COURAGE AND THE TRIUMPHAL ARCHES ERECTED BY A GENERAL OR THE COMMUNITY EXIST ONLY THROUGH THE MAGNITUDE OF THE MURDER. **St. Basil** (330–379)

Q. Is there anything else that occupies your time at this time?
A. There are lots of things. One of them...
Q. We know what you were doing April 2nd of 1999.
A. Yes. But there is a program that I'm involved in where we help people to go and live and work in third world countries, in very poor areas and really learn, first-hand about a different culture, and have a different class experience and then come home and begin to see how to apply that sort of thing. It's called One World and it's a global education program. So I have a lot of energy in that also.

ONE COULD UNDERGO THE ENTIRE CHRISTIAN INDUCTION, THE SEASONAL RHYTHMS OF CHRISTIAN WORSHIP, COULD RECEIVE THE CHRISTIAN SACRAMENTS; COULD BE EXPOSED YEAR AFTER YEAR TO ELITE CHRISTIAN EDUCATION. AND STILL ONE WOULD GO OFF TO WAR, IN APPARENT GOOD CONSCIENCE. **Daniel Berrigan**, *To Dwell in Peace*

WITH ALL THOSE PEOPLE DYING *FOR* THE REGIME, IT IS HIGH TIME SOMEONE DIED *AGAINST* IT. 21-year-old **Sophie Scholl** of the *White Rose* resistance movement; she, her brother and other university students were beheaded by the Nazis for leafleting the German people in an effort to expose the government's lies and to break the paralysis of fear.

Q. Sending your people from Canada to third world countries?

Q. Thank you. Now, what is your recollection of the events on April 2nd, 1999?

A. Much the same as has been described by Reverend Heap and Len Desroches. Where do you want me to start…

THE COURT: So you're basically in agreement with what has been said by both co-accused?

THE WITNESS: Yes, I am.

MR. SALVATERRA:

Q. Perhaps you can start a little bit with your purpose. I mean, why did you engage in what you said you engaged in?

The reason it took two and a half years is because we know that the churches had to hear that message, that that's blasphemous.

The urgency is real and what we did needed to be done and needs to be continued — not that we need to go back to the sword and the cross again, but the larger question of renouncing war.

I am absolutely convinced that one of the most important teachings of Jesus Christ is to love your enemy and that if you actually try to practice that, that there is no way that you can justify violence or war. It is not possible. We have a God who loves us unconditionally. This was Jesus' gospel, and he calls us to the same love. The cross especially exemplifies it.

What happened in Iraq with the bombing is just the beginning. There are 67 wars going on right now, live ones, on this planet at this moment. I mean, the urgency for the churches to speak out and disown war as a legitimate means of solving a conflict it's... it's beyond urgent. It's mandatory!

A. Very good. I am absolutely convinced that one of the most important teachings of Jesus Christ is to love your enemy, and that if you actually practice that there is no way that you can justify violence or war. It's not possible. We have a God who loves us unconditionally. This was Jesus' gospel, and he calls us to that same love. The cross especially exemplifies it.

Jesus, in the agony in the garden, had a choice. He could run or he could stand up and fight. He didn't. And so the cross represents that unconditional love of enemy, even to the point of forgiving those that are executing you. So it is the sign, the symbol of unconditional love and love of enemy. When Jesus was arrested, Peter took out his sword and started swinging it around. He was going to defend Jesus and Jesus said to him, "Put it away". And I really believe in my heart that he was saying that to each one of us, everybody who is his follower, "Put down the sword. That's not the way".

(Left to Right) Peter Rosenthal, Don Heap, David McComb and Sil Salvaterra in the courthouse corridor

EITHER JESUS WAS A LIAR, OR WAR IS NEVER NECESSARY.

> **Benjamin Salmon**, U.S. Catholic conscientious objector to World War I; he was given the death penalty which was commuted to a 25-year sentence; during his sentence he endured torture, solitary confinement and commitment to a mental hospital before being released.

To have a public monument on Bloor Street that everybody sees with an instrument of war, a sword on the cross of Jesus is…well, I haven't burst out crying like Len did, but that's how I feel. My heart just sinks, because that is blasphemy. That's not the gospel. That's not what Jesus taught and the sword has got to come off because it's a lie. It's just a symbol though. If we took the sword off and went on with life, if nothing changed, then that's not enough.

> WAR ITSELF IS A LIE. WE NEED TO ORGANIZE PEACE AS MEN HAVE ORGANIZED WAR.
>
> **Max Josef Metzer**, Jesuit priest, executed by Hitler's Gestapo

The reason it took two and a half years is because we know that the churches had to hear the message that this is blasphemous. That's why we spent all that time trying to contact the six mainline churches, and vigiling in front of them and had monthly vigils in front of the sword and the cross. We did all these things to bring that to people's attention, that it had to be changed, and to ask them over and over again to change it. And on Good Friday, the feast of the cross, we said we will start that process.

Q. The words that you used were to put it away, and in dialogue with the church…
A. M'hmm.
Q. …was that what you were suggesting?
A. In dialogue with the church, first with St. Paul's, and then with Bishop Finlay and then with the wider community; we wanted someone to take the initiative to take the sword off all the crosses in the sense of renouncing war and violence as a way, as a force, as Len would say, and choosing nonviolence as the way. That's our real aim.
Q. If they had chosen to put it away, as you put it, the churches…

A. M'hmm.

Q. ...what would your response have been?

A. We would have been delighted if they had done that, and we hoped it would have been very widely noted and celebrated if they had taken off the sword. Always, though, we were trying to enhance that monument, because we wanted that sword melted down and beaten into a ploughshare—as the Prophet Isaiah said—and mounted back up. In fact, we said, "You take it off and give it to us and we will pay for an artist to do that and put it back up".

> WAR DEFILES THIS WORLD,
> BUT DEATH IN GOD RENEWS IT.
> **T. S. Eliot**, *Murder in the Cathedral*

Q. Now, in this process of dialogue that you've spoken about, how, in effect, did you hope to achieve what was set out as your stated purpose?

A. Well, the discussions had been going on for a long time and nothing was happening. So by saying we were going to do this if you don't [take the sword off the cross], we added the urgency that we felt in our hearts, and there is not the slightest doubt how urgent it is. I mean, right now our oceans have got submarines sailing around under them with trident missiles that can blow the world apart. It's urgent that the churches speak out and say no to war right now. Long discussion groups and long years of writing papers weren't underlining the urgency. Whereas the action has, indeed, done that.

> THE HONEST HISTORIAN WILL HAVE SOME BITTER THINGS TO SAY ABOUT THE CONTRIBUTION OF THE CHURCHES TO THE CREATION OF THE MASS MIND. **Alfred Delp**, Jesuit priest, executed by the Nazis.

Q. You speak of this urgency and this sort of imminent danger.

A. M'hmm.

Q. The previous witness gave the analogy of a burning house and saving children from it. I mean, does that make sense to you?

A. Oh, it makes much sense and it's much...it's much greater than a house that's on fire. The danger of the conflagration is immense. I mean, what happened in Iraq with the bombing is just the beginning, and now the sanctions are having incredible effects. There are 67 wars going on right now, live ones, on this planet at this moment. I mean, the urgency for the churches to speak out and disown war as a legitimate means of solving conflict it's, it's beyond urgent. It's mandatory. We've got to do it right away.

Q. And how could you possibly believe that removing or bending a sword from a cross could prevent that kind of imminent danger, or begin to?

A. By raising the awareness of the churches. [That's why] we'd written to the bishops and the leaders of all the mainline churches here in Toronto. And I have to say Bishop Finlay, the Anglican bishop, has responded well and yesterday we had such a discussion. Again, it was only discussion, but it was a good start.

Q. So you had discussions. Is that further than what occurred prior to yesterday?

A. Yeah. The discussions before that we had with Bishop Finlay, in Holy Week last year, centered on the cross at St. Paul's.

Q. The previous witness was asked and I'll ask you as well: Do you believe you had, in your understanding, a lawful right to do what you did?

A. Absolutely, absolutely. I, too, was arrested at the Innu situation, so I'm very aware of the law allowing necessity in that case. I really agree with Bishop Gumbleton, that the law that protects property is not the widest or deepest or greatest law. The law that protects persons is far, far, far more important. What we did was to [try to] protect persons from war, and from having their minds think that it's okay for Christians to fight wars. The law would certainly allow the protection of persons in my mind. I have no hesitancy here at all.

> MEXICAN SOLDIER, WE HAVE ASKED FOR THE DEMILITARIZATION OF THE REGION BUT THE GOVERNMENT DOESN'T LISTEN. WE NOW ASK YOU TO LEAVE THE MILITARY CAMP. DON'T SHED THE BLOOD OF YOUR BROTHERS AND SISTERS BECAUSE WHEN YOU KILL A PERSON, YOU ARE KILLING GOD.

Las Abejas (The Bees), a pacifist, indigenous organization in Chiapas Mexico. *Christian Peacemaker Teams* (CPT) has a presence in Chiapas.

WE SAY 'NO' TO INJUSTICE. WE DON'T CARRY ARMS OR PARTICIPATE WITH ANY ARMED ACTORS.

Sign nailed to two tree branches at the entrance of one of the peace communities who are risking their lives in war-torn Columbia

WE ARE CALLED THE "LOST BOYS OF SUDAN"... OUR FAMILIES AND VILLAGES HAVE BEEN DESTROYED BY WAR. WE HAVE WALKED A THOUSAND MILES IN SUDAN, ETHIOPIA AND KENYA. FOR FOURTEEN YEARS WE HAVE SUFFERED TERRIBLE HARDSHIPS, SUCH THAT AT LEAST HALF OF OUR ORIGINAL NUMBER HAVE DIED...WE EARNESTLY DESIRE PEACE, NOT REVENGE. WE WANT NO MORE WEAPONS KILLING ANY OF OUR SUDANESE BROTHERS AND SISTERS, FROM THE NORTH OF SUDAN OR FROM THE SOUTH OF SUDAN. ALL OF US WERE CREATED BY ONE GOD, AND IT IS TIME FOR US TO FORGIVE AND EMBRACE EACH OTHER.

Lost Boys' *Call for Peace,* September 2001

Q. The war memorial is purportedly in front of St. Paul's, or near St. Paul's?
A. M'hmm.
Q. How far on April 2nd, did you finally go before being arrested?
A. Well, we were told that if we went over the fence we'd be arrested and charged with trespass, and that's exactly what happened.
Q. Precisely how far...
A. We weren't charged with trespass.
Q. Yes.

A. We were charged with mischief when we got to 52 Division.

Q. Can you just describe very briefly what that moment consisted of at the fence?

A. Yes. I'm the mountain climber, so I went first. We had made two small ladders that went to the top of the fence. We put one on the other side first by lifting it over [the fence] and then we put one on our side so we could just walk up one side and down the other. Before I could even start up [the ladder] on my side [of the fence], the police, who were inside the [fenced-in] compound, took away the inside ladder. I pleaded for them to put it back—not for my sake but we're not all as spry as I—and they wouldn't. When I climbed down on the inside I was immediately arrested.

Q. Thank you. Those are my questions. Thank you, Your Honour.

THE COURT: Thank you.

CROSS EXAMINATION BY MR. ROSENTHAL:

Q. Sir, you told us now that you were instructed by the police that you might be arrested for trespass if you climbed over that fence, is that correct?

A. Yes, m'hmm.

Q. You were in court when the officer said that he said trespass and mischief. He's mistaken in that, is he?

A. I can only say what I heard. I never heard the word mischief and he certainly didn't say that when we got in the paddy wagon. We didn't hear mischief until we had been separated and locked up in 52 Division, I think, for almost two hours before they came in and charged us with mischief.

Q. You had heard trespass prior to that time?

A. Well, we presumed it was trespass.

Q. But someone had told you trespass, didn't they?

A. They told us trespass before we went over the fence. That's all.

Q. Now, you've told us that you felt a sense of urgency about doing this, and you explained why. After two times I can anticipate perhaps a question from the crown as to why, if it was so urgent, why did you wait until Good Friday? Why didn't you do it before then?

A. That's a good question. Because when the Gulf War was… they were rattling the sabres again in February of '98, we really did want to go and do it right away, as a sign and symbol. But we realized that a dialogue needed to be had with St. Paul's, and then as we got into that dialogue we realized that we needed to carry this dialogue to the other churches, but we still needed to underline the urgency by setting a date and saying, "If you can't bring yourself to do it, then we will have to do it."

> AS I REFLECT ON THE HARD DECISIONS PEOPLE ARE MAKING TODAY WITH REGARD TO ACTIONS AND CONSEQUENCES, I REALIZE WE ARE—ALL OF US—BEGINNERS—NO MORE, NO LESS.
>
> **Elizabeth McAlister**, in *Maternal Convictions*

Q. And in setting the date on Good Friday, did you hope that because of the symbolic value of Good Friday it would have greater impact?
A. Absolutely, yeah. It was the perfect date.
Q. Thank you, sir. Thank you, Your Honour.
THE COURT: I think that today the priests have taken first place over the lawyers as effective speakers and I hope the lawyers are now going to try to regain first place on their submissions. We're going to put this over to the 19th in 125 court, 10:00 a.m.

THE JUDGEMENT

THE ONTARIO COURT OF JUSTICE
HER MAJESTY THE QUEEN
against
LEONARD DESROCHES, DANIEL HEAP AND ROBERT HOLMES

> I SAID "I DON'T KNOW HOW TO SPEAK." GOD REPLIED "THERE! I AM PUTTING MY WORDS INTO YOUR MOUTH."
> **Jeremiah** (1:6&9)

SENTENCE HEARING

BEFORE THE HONOURABLE MR. JUSTICE C.H. PARIS
On June 19th, 2000, at Toronto.

> KILLING ONE PERSON IN A JUNGLE IS AN UNFORGIVABLE CRIME. KILLING AN ENTIRE NATION IS A MATTER FOR CONSIDERATION.
>
> **Abdul Rahman Kawkabi**, early 20th century Arab poet
>
> THE WORLD IS AT A CROSSROADS. IT HAS TO MAKE ITS CHOICE BETWEEN THE LAW OF THE JUNGLE AND THE LAW OF HUMANITY. **Gandhi**

> We intended to address a very destructive symbol: the imposition of the sword on the cross is a very clear message that the cross of itself is not a force; that when we have enemies, we need the force of the sword.
>
> The symbol of the sword on the cross perpetuates warfare.
>
> Unless we come to terms as a church with our role in warfare nothing will change and wars will be perpetuated.
>
> We felt it was a moral imperative for the church to do something beyond words, beyond statements, about the renunciation of the institution of war.

CHARGE: Attempt to cause mischief

APPEARANCES:

Counsel for the Crown	E. Carrington, Esq.
Counsel for the Accused L. Desroches	P. McComb, Esq.
Counsel for the Accused D. Heap	P. Rosenthal, Esq.

> FROM PAUL, A PRISONER OF CHRIST JESUS, TO OUR DEAR FELLOW WORKER PHILEMON, OUR SISTER APPHIA AND THE CHURCH THAT MEETS IN YOUR HOUSE. I PRAY THAT [YOUR] FAITH WILL GIVE RISE TO A SENSE OF FELLOWSHIP THAT WILL SHOW YOU ALL THE GOOD THINGS THAT WE ARE ABLE TO DO FOR CHRIST. EPAPHRAS, A PRISONER WITH ME IN CHRIST JESUS, SENDS HIS GREETINGS. MAY THE GRACE OF JESUS CHRIST BE WITH YOUR SPIRIT. Letter to Philemon.

> GOING TO JAIL, DOING CIVIL DISOBEDIENCE, ISN'T ALL THAT SPECIAL OR THREATENING. IT'S JUST SOMETHING THAT HAS TO BE DONE IN A WORLD WHERE INSANITY IS LEGAL. CIVIL DISOBEDIENCE IS A FACT OF LIFE. I HOPE WE LEARN TO ACCEPT IT GRACEFULLY. **Shelley Douglass**

MR. CARRINGTON: Good morning, Your Honour. I was hoping we could deal with the matter of Messrs. Heap, Holmes and Desroches at the beginning, as I'm required to be in 122 court as well.

THE COURT: Okay.

CLERK OF THE COURT: The Crown's name?

MR. CARRINGTON: Carrington, initial E. for the record.

THE COURT: The three accused are charged with one count of attempt to commit mischief: Daniel Heap, Leonard Desroches and Robert Holmes have been involved in pacifist activities for a number of years.

On the premises of St. Paul's Anglican Church on Bloor Street East, Toronto, there is a war memorial. It consists of a large cross cut from a piece of granite with a sword affixed to it. The monument has been at this location since 1931 and is in the perpetual care of the Queen's Own Rifles Regiment.

The accused believe that the juxtaposition of a sword, a symbol of war, on a cross, a symbol of love and redemption, is blasphemy. They also believe that if they could convince the Anglican Church to remove the sword it would be a powerful anti-war statement. Their views are shared by some influential members of the traditional churches.

> GOD IS LOVE AND ANYONE WHO LIVES IN LOVE LIVES IN GOD, AND GOD IN THAT PERSON. IF YOU REFUSE TO LOVE, YOU REMAIN DEAD. ANYONE WHO SAYS "I LOVE GOD," AND HATES SISTER OR BROTHER IS A LIAR. OUR LOVE IS NOT TO BE JUST WORDS OR MERE TALK, BUT SOMETHING REAL AND ACTIVE. **First letter of John** (4:16; 3:15; 4:20; 3:18)

The accused used the monument as a catalyst for the creation of the Sword and Cross movement.

Its main goals are to see to the removal of the sword from the monument and the rejection of the Just War doctrine by the mainline Churches. For about 18 months, the movement organized vigils and meetings with Anglican Church officials where they discussed their concerns. Eventually, the Church decline to remove the sword although it agreed to discuss the Just War doctrine at its general meeting.

The accused then organized a demonstration for Good Friday, April 2, 1999, where, according to flyers, the sword would be removed. On April 2, the accused, accompanied by approximately 50 supporters, arrived at St. Paul's carrying two ladders, a prybar and several straps. They were met by about 30 police officers called in by parish officials. P.C. Elliot warned the accused that they would be arrested if they climbed the fence. They did and they were arrested for mischief. There was no disturbance or damage to property.

The accused raise the defence of excuse based on necessity and colour of right. In *Perka v. The Queen* 1984, 14 C.C.C. (3d) 385, the Supreme

Court of Canada held that the common law defence of necessity should be strictly controlled.

The priests felt that since the juxtaposition of the sword and the cross was blasphemy, they were duty-bound to remove the sword. This defence must fail for several reasons. The monument became an issue in 1997. There were vigils and meetings. The demonstration was organized well in advance. Symbolically it was scheduled for Good Friday. The flyers stated that there could be arrests during the demonstration.

This was not an emergency situation. Indeed, it was organized by the accused. There was no imminent peril to the accused that required an immediate response. There were legal alternatives to the decision to disobey the law. The issues were to be argued at the forum of the Anglican Church later. It was quite clear from the evidence of Mr. Heap, which was adopted by his co-accused, that they had simply grown impatient with the slow decision making process of the church. Impatience and frustration cannot be the basis to the defence of necessity.

> BREATHING THE AIR OR DRINKING THE WATER CAN BE HEALTH HAZARDS. SAFE SEWAGE TREATMENT DEMANDS A CONTINUOUS SOURCE OF POWER BUT THE HYDRO BLACKOUTS THAT OCCUR ALMOST DAILY DISCHARGE RAW SEWAGE INTO THE RIVER SYSTEM.
>
> IT REMAINS TO BE SEEN HOW CANADIANS WILL COPE WITH THEIR SENSE OF GUILT AND BETRAYAL BY OUR LEADERS ONCE THE IMMORAL SANCTIONS ARE UNIVERSALLY CONDEMNED AND NORTH AMERICANS LEARN THE TRUE HORROR OF THE GENOCIDE IN WHICH WE HAVE PARTICIPATED. **Carol Winter**, member of *Project Ploughshares* (Canada) and of a recent delegation to Iraq (*Toronto Star*, January 31, 2001)

The colour of right argument has two prongs. They argue that they held an honest belief that their action would enhance, not reduce, the value of the monument. They also argue that their action would cause the Churches to renounce the Just War doctrine, which could save lives in Iraq and Kosovo.

The accused intended to pry away the tip of the sword hoping that the church would then complete the removal. They felt that this would enhance the value of the monument as an anti-war symbol. The problem is that the owner of the monument did not agree. Bishop Finlay told them not to proceed with their plans. Officials of St. Paul's asked for the assistance of the police. P.C. Elliot, in the presence of these officials, warned the accused they would be arrested if they climbed the fence. The accused knew that the owners were asserting their rights to the property. In these circumstances, whether the value was enhanced or reduced, was irrelevant.

> PRIVATE PROPERTY DOES NOT CONSTITUTE, FOR ANYONE, AN ABSOLUTE RIGHT.
> **Pope Paul VI** in *Progressio Populorum*
> (On the Development of the Peoples)

In *R.v.V.* (M) 1998, 123 C.C.C. (3rd) 138, Mr. Justice Goudge for the Ontario Court of Appeal held that if there is some evidence of real physical damage to the property, the Crown is not required to establish that it has been reduced in value. In this case, there was an intention to cause real physical damage to the monument. The defence, therefore, must fail.

They finally argue that because the accused honestly believed that their action would convince the Churches to renounce the Just War doctrine, it had a potential to save lives in Iraq and Kosovo. The ends here justified the means. Therefore, they had a colour of right to act as they did.

In *R.v.Watson* the Newfoundland Court of Appeal quoted with approval the following portion of the trial judge's charge to the jury: "…'the colour of right' as a defence cannot apply unless a mistake is honestly held by the accused. Thus, the first step you must consider [is] whether there is evidence indicating that the accused believed that he was authorized to do what he did by the World Charter, and that that believe was honestly held."

As seen previously, the accused were told repeatedly by different people representing the owners of the monument that they could not remove the sword. In one of their flyers they acknowledged that there could be some arrests during the demonstration. They acted in full knowledge of circumstances, and therefore they cannot now claim that they acted pursuant to an honestly held mistake.

> WHEN THEY HAD BROUGHT THEM IN TO FACE THE SANHEDRIN, THE HIGH PRIEST DEMANDED AN EXPLANATION. "WE GAVE YOU A FORMAL WARNING" HE SAID, "NOT TO PREACH IN THIS NAME, AND WHAT HAVE YOU DONE?"
>
> IN REPLY PETER AND THE APOSTLES SAID, "OBEDIENCE TO GOD COMES BEFORE OBEDIENCE TO HUMANS."
>
> **Acts of the early church** (5:27–29)

They claimed that their actions were justified because they could save lives in Iraq and Kosovo. Mr. Heap, again speaking for the three, testified that he was not sure that their actions would have the desired effect, but it was the only thing he could think of at the time. This falls short of the requirement for a successful use of the defences of colour of right or necessity as set above.

During submissions, Mr. Carrington referred to the decision of my brother, Mr. Justice Cole, in *R.v.Clarke*. This case is particularly helpful, not only because it deals with the same legal issues, but the facts themselves are very similar.

In *Clarke* the accused are social activists who organized a demonstration at a boarded-up building in order to publicize the plight of the homeless. They were met by a police officer who warned them not to enter the premises. The two accused then, using a prybar, tried to remove a board from a window. Mr. Justice Cole found that the defences of necessity and colour of right, and the defence that there was no damage done, were not available. I agree fully with his analysis and, to the extent that his reasons are applicable to this case, I incorporate them as part of my judgment.

For these reasons I find the accused guilty…

> WHY DO WE CONDEMN AND HANG INDIVIDUAL KILLERS WHILE EXTOLLING THE VIRTUES OF WARMONGERS…IN A SYSTEM THAT OPERATES IN SUCH A MANNER AS TO PROVIDE ONE TYPE OF JUSTICE FOR THE RICH AND A LESSER TYPE FOR THE POOR; ONE STANDARD FOR THE MIGHTY AND ANOTHER FOR THE MEEK; WHICH FINDS ITS HUMANNESS AND OBJECTIVITY SUBLIMATED TO MILITARY MADNESS AND THE WORSHIP OF THE BOMB?
>
> **U.S. Judge Miles Lord**, as he handed down a suspended sentence to two people who had damaged a Trident nuclear submarine component (November 8, 1984, Minneapolis)

> YOU ARE DOOMED WHO MAKE UNJUST LAWS; WHO DEPRIVE THE WEAKEST OF MY PEOPLE OF JUSTICE; WHO CALL EVIL GOOD AND GOOD EVIL. IS IT NOTHING TO YOU THAT YOU GRIND THE FACES OF THE POOR? NO MATTER HOW MUCH YOU PRAY, YOUR HANDS ARE COVERED WITH BLOOD.
>
> **Isaiah** (10:1–2; 5:20; 3:15; 1:15)

MR. ROSENTHAL: We had intended to present to Your Honour, on sentencing, two letters that we have received with respect to sentencing. This is a letter from Philip Berrigan, and he begins:

> My name is Philip Berrigan, a married Catholic priest, who has for 35 years withstood non-violently American war-making. For my pains, I've been rewarded with nine years of imprisonment—first for resistance to the Vietnam War, and then the nuclear arms race. I write from prison.

And then he describes then the action that led to his being in prison this particular time. To save the court's time, I don't intend to read the entire letter, but I would like to emphasize a paragraph about two thirds of the way down, where Reverend Berrigan writes:

> Why is the U.S. constantly at war, with Canada a ready and willing accomplice? One reason would be the Christian skill at tradeoffs: the Established Church trades to Caesar its moral neutrality for tax exemption and other perks; the individual Christian trades to Caesar taxes and silence for a six-fold share of the world's goods and services. For most Christians, there is really no other King but Caesar.
>
> Not so with Len Desroches, Don Heap and Bob Holmes. They are Christians of a different stripe. They know that the Cross stands irrevocably against the sword, guns and bombs. They also know that there will be no peace without justice.

I'm just reading that excerpt for Your Honour. You have the entire letter before you.

We have one other letter that is headed the Church of St. John the Evangelist. This is an Anglican Church in Ottawa. On the front page of that is a sort of cover letter about the letter, signed by the rector of that church, where he indicates that some seven or eight persons listed there have endorsed the matter which follows on the second page.

This, you'll note, is dated on May 15, 2000, which was the time that we appeared before Your Honour on the trial itself.

This is headed: "An open letter of support for those affirming the nonviolence of Jesus from some members of the Anglican Diocese of Ottawa." And it describes the event of the attempt to remove the sword and the purpose of the action. And then it states, beginning about two-thirds of the way down the page,

> We, the undersigned, wish to express our gratitude to these Christian activists for courageously insisting that the Christian church look at the ways in which it condones violence, especially in armed conflict against other nations.

THE *CANADIAN RELIGIOUS CONFERENCE* REPRESENTING THE PRIESTS, BROTHERS AND

SISTERS CONSECRATED BY VOWS TO THE SERVICE OF GOD'S PEOPLE, JOINS WITH YOU IN PRAYER.

MAY THE SPIRIT OF THE GOD OF JESUS THAT CALLS US TO SPEAK THE TRUTH, WHATEVER THE CONSEQUENCES, GUIDE AND STRENGTHEN YOU AS YOU TRY TO BRING THE MESSAGE THAT THE OUTRAGE OF WAR CANNOT IN ANY WAY BE RECONCILED TO THE GOOD NEWS OF THE GOSPEL.

Richard Renshaw, CSC, Assistant Secretary General of the *Canadian Religious Conference*

IN THIS TIME OF JUBILEE THE WHOLE WORLD IS HOPING FOR A NEW BEGINNING—A BEGINNING THAT CAN ONLY BE REALIZED WITH AN END TO POVERTY, HOMELESSNESS AND EVERY FORM OF VIOLENCE.

WHICH IS THE GREATER CRIMINAL ACT—MILITARISM AND ITS EFFECTS OR THE RESISTANCE TO IT?

The staff and community of *The Lantern*, a Christian life centre in St. John's Newfoundland

LOOKING BACK TO THE 20TH CENTURY THAT HAS JUST COME TO A CLOSE, HUMANITY HAS WITNESSED THE MOST DEVASTATING WARS EVER EXPERIENCED. CHRISTIANS HAVE PLAYED AN IMPORTANT ROLE IN THIS DRAMATIC SITUATION. WE HAVE BETRAYED THE TRUE "REVOLUTION" THAT CHRIST REVEALED TO OUR WORLD: THE ABSOLUTE RESPECT OF THE HUMAN BEING—FRIEND OR ENEMY—AND THE POWER OF JUSTICE, TRUTH, LOVE AND ACTIVE

NONVIOLENCE TO OVERCOME EVIL IN ALL ITS FORMS.

Dr. Hildegard Goss-Mayr, Honorary President, International Fellowship of Reconciliation

LOVE OF ENEMY, PROPERLY UNDERSTOOD, IS OUR ONLY HOPE IN A WORLD FILLED WITH CONFLICT AND HATRED.

Mary-Ellen Francoeur, Sisters of Service

THE ONLY CHANCE FOR THE SURVIVAL OF THE NEXT FEW GENERATIONS IS THAT WE LEARN THE JOY OF CARING AND SHARING; FORGIVING AND ACCEPTING ALL THE PEOPLE IN THE WORLD.

Muriel Luca, an elder in Canada's peace movement

I understand that each of [the defendants] would like to make a brief statement to Your Honour. And then I would just summarize that position. The first person would be Mr. Desroches.

MR. DESROCHES: Outside the quiet of this courtroom I know that there are two major things going on. One of them is the day-to-day brutalizing of the world through militarism. It's something that's too obvious—the impoverishment and the starvation of people in the world through militarism that goes on day by day; Canada's own participation in the killing of over a million people in Iraq.

The other thing that's going on that we hear much less about is the renunciation, not just of wars, but of the Institution of War. And I'd like to cite two examples. Recently I was quite privileged to be asked to address religious leaders from across Canada in the Roman Catholic community—the leaders of communities such as Franciscans, Jesuits and so forth, all of the religious communities from coast to coast, 300 of them.

There was a unanimous acceptance of the urgent need to renounce not just wars but the Institution of War itself; and to renounce the false teaching of the Just War.

The second example that's also not been well publicized is the UN's declaration of this decade as a decade for the building of a culture of nonviolence.

I really believe that laws are meant to change. The support for slavery was once written in law till there was an abolition movement. I think the new abolition movement is the movement for the abolition of war itself, of the Institution of War.

In closing, I would like to read two or three sentences from a judge, because at this late stage of the process I obviously don't have any hopes at all of changing the court's mind, even though I fundamentally disagree that this was not an urgent issue. Purely on the matter of urgency I think we should have been found not guilty.

> WE ARE IN THE PROCESS OF DESTROYING AN ENTIRE SOCIETY. IT IS AS SIMPLE AND AS TERRIFYING AS THAT. IT IS ILLEGAL AND IMMORAL.
>
> **Dennis Halliday**, former UN Oil-for-Food coordinator, at his resignation speech, September 30, 1998

I'd like to quote Judge Ulf Panzer, a German judge. In 1997, he and 20 judges committed civil disobedience against war. They were arrested. They did a blockade in front of a U.S. nuclear missile base in Germany. When Judge Panzer wrote me a letter, he also sent me the statement he read when he appeared before a brother judge. I'll read from the judge's statement:

> What did bring me to do this? Just because I wanted to do a little act of violence? What made me take the stress of a criminal trial, of the disciplinary action yet to come, the uncertainty of whether I can keep my job? Finding us guilty, as you intend to do, means legalizing a crime. German judges have a long history of legalizing crimes, Mr. Judge.
>
> THE EXTERMINATION OF THE JEWS DID NOT SUIT YOU. AS FOR RELIGION, [THE GOVERNMENT] SAYS: PLEASE TAKE CARE OF THAT AS YOU PLEASE;

> ONLY STAY IN THE OTHER WORLD WITH YOUR DEMANDS, CHURCH. OTHERWISE THE CHURCH COULD CONCERN ITSELF WITH POLITICS. WE FIGHT ON. THE ARMED FORCES VOICE THEIR SALUTE: HEIL, HITLER! WE ALL VOICE THE SALUTE: HEIL, HITLER! WITH TOTAL STRENGTH, WE MARCH TOWARD THE FINAL VICTORY.
>
> **Dr. Roland Freisler**, President of *the People's Court*, as he sentenced to death those who had opposed the Führer
>
> You're going to protect injustice against the people. May I remind you that your job is to protect people against injustices.

And then he ends by saying, "I guess you don't have the courage to say no to injustice. You have my understanding, Mr. Judge. It took me a long time to find that courage".

My plea is that the court send some signal for the need for laws themselves to change, to enhance an abolition movement against the institution of war itself.

> THE INSTITUTION OF SLAVERY HAS RECEIVED THE SANCTION OF THE ALMIGHTY IN THE PATRIARCHAL AGE…IT WAS INCORPORATED INTO THE ONLY NATIONAL CONSTITUTION WHICH EVER EMANATED FROM GOD…IT'S LEGALITY WAS RECOGNIZED AND ITS RELATIVE DUTIES REGULATED, BY JESUS CHRIST IN HIS KINGDOM.
>
> **Reverend Thornton Stringfellow**, in *Slavery Defended: The Views of the Old South*, Eric L. McKitirck, ed. (Prentice Hall, 1963)
>
> I WILL OPPOSE [SLAVERY] WITH ALL THE MORAL POWER WITH WHICH I AM ENDOWED. I AM NOT AN ADVOCATE OF PASSIVITY. **Lucretia Mott**, 19th

century U.S. Quaker who participated in the successful abolition movement against the institution of slavery and who worked against the institution of war and for the rights of women

WAR IS AS OUTMODED AS CANNIBALISM, CHATTEL SLAVERY, BLOOD-FEUDS, AND DUELLING, AN INSULT TO GOD AND HUMANITY; A DAILY CRUCIFIXION OF CHRIST.

Muriel Lester (1883–1968), co-founder of *Kingsley Hall* in the impoverished East End of London, England; for the last thirty years of her life, she circled the globe as secretary of the International Fellowship of Reconciliation.

MR. ROSENTHAL: Mr. Heap is next, sir.

MR. HEAP: Your Honour, I wish to make two points. And I've listened carefully to your reasons. My first point is that although we spent more than a year asking the local and the diocesan areas to take action or to announce an action, for renouncing war and dealing with a blasphemous use of the sword on that monument, before Good Friday of 1999 there was no sign on action.

The fact that the General Synod the year before had called for a general discussion in Anglican parishes was undermined by the fact that no preparation for that discussion was made after the Synod. No preparation for discussion has yet been made in any public way.

What was asked by that motion was to open the discussion, rather than to keep it closed until the next triennial Synod. And when Bishop Finlay wrote to me asking me not to do our action because he felt it would only polarize the discussion within the church, my answer was—and this is perhaps not exactly reflected in the record—but my answer was that there had been 17 or 18 centuries, not months, centuries of discussion within the church since the Emperor Constantine made a pact with the bishops.

THE RADICAL TRUTHS OF THE FAITH BECOME REALLY TRUE AND REALLY RADICAL WHEN THE CHURCH ENTERS INTO THE LIFE AND DEATH

> OF ITS PEOPLE. THEN THERE IS PUT BEFORE THE FAITH OF THE CHURCH, AS IT IS PUT BEFORE THE FAITH OF EVERY INDIVIDUAL, THE MOST FUNDAMENTAL CHOICE: TO BE IN FAVOUR OF LIFE OR TO BE IN FAVOUR OF DEATH. **Archbishop Oscar Romero**

And the basis of the discussion is, "We'll go on killing our enemies, but we'll discuss whether we should stop killing our enemies." So there has been no change in that practice. My second point is—and I will say to my surprise—an event occurred the day before the trial. Not before our action on Good Friday, but this year, the day before the trial, when Bishop Finlay chaired a debate in open forum in the parish of All Saints on Sunday afternoon, the 14th of May, on the question of, "Can a war be just?"

I had never heard of that question being opened publicly by a bishop. I've asked my friends, they've never heard of it. That is something new, something I welcome with all my heart. But that had not happened before Good Friday of 1999.

I do not challenge, Your Honour, your interpretation of the law. But I want to say that at this moment I continue to be very happy with the choice that I made…and very happy with the response which I think has been brought partly by our action.

> LET THE DREAM OF CHRIST BE IN US.
> from the hymn *Draw the Circle Wide*, by **Gordon Light**, Anglican priest.

MR. ROSENTHAL: And Father Holmes.

MR. HOLMES: Good morning, Your Honour. I too want to say that I am relatively content with the results of our symbolic action. I think we have indeed raised the consciousness of the mainline churches. We've raised the question of how appropriate or inappropriate it is to put a sword on a cross; and the larger question of the churches blessing war. I think those questions have been raised, and I'm very happy with that.

I too see some signs of hope. The U.S. bishops in their peace pastoral a few years ago, recognized within the Roman Catholic denomination that the rejection of all war, the renunciation of all war, is a very legitimate Catholic stance in faith.

> LOVE IS NOT STARVING OF WHOLE POPULATIONS. LOVE IS NOT THE BOMBARDMENT OF OPEN CITIES. LOVE IS NOT KILLING. IT IS THE LAYING DOWN OF ONE'S LIFE.
>
> THERE IS NOTHING THAT WE CAN DO BUT LOVE, AND DEAR GOD—PLEASE ENLARGE OUR HEARTS TO LOVE EACH OTHER, TO LOVE OUR NEIGHBOUR, TO LOVE OUR ENEMY AS WELL AS OUR FRIEND. **Dorothy Day**

Our present pope has condemned all the recent wars there have been, and is moving in that direction towards condemning all war, I believe. So I think our action is one step along that line.

I too disagree when you say that there's no urgency or imminence that required our action. I think there is an incredible urgency, now more than ever.

Yesterday I was in Hamilton at the war show and watched as people just ohhed and ahhed over the military planes and destructive capability that our countries have. I was in tears, to be truthful.

> YOU ARE WELL AWARE, MY BROTHERS AND SISTERS, THAT WE ARE SUFFICIENTLY FEEBLE TO TRIGGER OFF THE THIRD AND FINAL WORLD WAR.
>
> YOU KNOW AS WELL THAT WE ARE SUFFICIENTLY STRONG TO WIPE AWAY FROM THE SAME EARTH EVER MORE ITS MISERY. **Dom Helder Camara**

So the urgency is real and what we did needed to be done and needs to be continued—not that we need to go back to the sword and the cross again—but the larger question of renouncing war.

> FAR FROM BEING THE PIOUS INJUNCTION OF A UTOPIAN DREAMER, THE COMMAND TO LOVE ONE'S ENEMY IS AN ABSOLUTE NECESSITY FOR OUR SURVIVAL. WE ARE CALLED TO THIS DIFFICULT TASK IN ORDER TO REALIZE A UNIQUE RELATIONSHIP WITH GOD. **Martin Luther King**

I'd like to thank you and the court for allowing us to present a full discussion of our motivations and the reasons in this public forum. Thank you.

THE COURT: Yes.

MR. ROSENTHAL: Your Honour, I would suggest that there is no need for any condition on these gentlemen. The discharge should be absolute. They will not make any further attempts on that sword. If Your Honour does intend to impose some condition that would prohibit them from attending many other places on Bloor Street, it would be inappropriate.

If Your Honour feels that you must impose a condition of keeping them off that church property, then Your Honour may do so. In my respectful submission, their word is much more powerful than any possible condition may be.

THE COURT: Okay, thank you. During the trial on several occasions I mentioned that I did not doubt the good intentions of the accused in this case, that they truly believed in their calling, and they felt that this was the way to achieve what they were trying to achieve.

> EVERYTHING THAT IS NOW COVERED WILL BE UNCOVERED, AND EVERYTHING NOW HIDDEN WILL BE MADE CLEAR. WHAT I SAY TO YOU IN THE DARK, TELL IN THE DAYLIGHT; WHAT YOU HEAR IN WHISPERS, PROCLAIM FROM THE HOUSETOPS.
>
> **Jesus** (Mt. 10:26–7)

But when you live in a society there are limits to freedom because everyone has the freedom. Therefore, there will be clashes between different persons. I could not allow a person who is pro-war, for example [to have] absolute freedom, because that would clash with yours. And for that reason, you cannot have perfect freedom in a society. Or absolute freedom in a society.

> THE TRUTH WILL SET YOU FREE. **Jesus**

The church had a legitimate right to the property of the monument, and had a right to protect it. And for that reason, my interpretations made by other courts, other judges, is that the conduct was against the provisions of the Criminal Code.

I am not a political scientist. I am not a moralist. I am a judge whose job is to do the proper interpretation of the law. And that is how I came to the decision that your conduct was in breach of a section of the Criminal Code.

> IF YOU, EVEN YOU, HAD ONLY RECOGNIZED ON THIS DAY THE THINGS THAT MAKE FOR PEACE. **Jesus**

I hope you will forgive my language, but it seems from that meeting with Bishop Finlay that you may have won a battle on the way to winning the war.

I grant to each of you an absolute discharge.

> PEACE I LEAVE YOU. I DO NOT GIVE PEACE THE WAY THE WORLD GIVES IT. **Jesus**

> YOU HAVE LEARNT HOW IT WAS SAID: YOU MUST LOVE YOUR NEIGHBOUR, AND HATE YOUR ENEMY. BUT I SAY THIS TO YOU: LOVE YOUR ENEMIES
>
> **Jesus** (Matt. 5:43–44)

> BECOME AS MATURE IN LOVE AS GOD IS.
> **Jesus** (Matt. 5:48)

4 Prison walls, church walls and freedom

Personal reflections on the aftermath

Prison walls

"Oh, no!" You're going up against Smith. Man, you don't stand a chance!" exclaims one prisoner. The other responds, "Yeah, I'd give anything to appear before *your* judge."

In jail I quickly learned from the knowledgeable repeat offenders about which judge was compassionate and which one was brutal; about how arbitrary the system really is. Some judges have deep contempt for the "scum" brought before them. Some are more "liberal" and see the accused purely as victims to be "helped." Fewer have the radical spiritual wisdom and compassion to respect whoever appears before them as a brother or sister who is either wounded, lost, falsely accused or simply a resister to unjust laws.

During the Cross and Sword Trial, we were dealing with a judge who was both judicious (not all judges are), and unafraid to allow the fullness of the political and moral arguments to be put before the court (few judges allow that). Judge Paris did not accept the challenge which I presented to him: I urged him to take the same risk as Judge Ulf Panzer and the other German judges, who were arrested a few years ago for their refusal to cooperate with U.S. militarism on their soil. One way for Judge Paris to take up his responsibility to resist war would have been to dismiss the charges by agreeing that non-cooperation with war is urgent, and therefore justifiable according to the defence of necessity. And yet, I do believe that Judge Paris was deeply affected by the truthfulness of the words spoken in his courtroom on May 15, 2000. I believe that granting us an absolute discharge was his way of at least making a genuine personal statement—without taking the rare risks of resistance exemplified by the German judges.

"Absolute discharge" is a uniquely Canadian animal: you are found guilty of a criminal offence, but suffer no real legal consequences. The three of us had fully accepted the possibility of jail time. It is not an honest action if one doesn't fully accept the legal consequences. For me, the writing of this book has been my way of using this time of relative freedom responsibly. In fact, I believe that those of us who are committed to nonviolent resistance for the long haul need to take seriously the particular task we are called to do at a particular time. It is sometimes much easier to avoid the hard discipline of honest writing (article or book) and to busy ourselves with resistance for the sake of resistance. Only we can make that judgement—with all the wisdom, honesty and freedom possible.

All of us who were directly involved in the Cross and Sword Trial persist in our resistance to injustice and violence. Peter Rosenthal has been busy defending individuals involved in a range of issues related to social justice. Likewise for Sil Salvaterra and David McComb.

Jeannie Loughrey is still the priest at All Saints. Janet Somerville's term as General Secretary of the Canadian Council of Churches expires October 1, 2002. Tom Gumbleton continues to witness as a bishop—both in his parish and in his persistent noncooperation with the brutal militarism of his government.

Cathy Crowe persists in advocating for the homeless and affordable housing with the "1% Solution". The members of *Las Abejas* endure, against great odds, living out the risks of gospel nonviolence in Chiapas.

Don Heap is keenly interested in deepening the Anglican Church's commitment to repentance and restitution in relation to Canada's First Nations. For Don, Canada's policy of forcibly assimilating the remnants of the native peoples was a product of the military conquest of Canada by the British. Along with his involvement in Holy Trinity Parish, Don supports the work of many groups such as the Toronto Disaster Relief Committee.

Bob Holmes has committed himself to a long-term period of service with Christian Peacemaker Teams (CPT). He first served in Hebron.

Together with Palestinian and Israeli peace workers, CPT seeks to reduce the physical and structural violence suffered by Palestinians at the hands of the Israeli security forces and settlers. Bob has also served briefly at Esgenoopetiji (Burnt Church), New Brunswick where the Mi'kmaqs claim the right to regulate their own fishery under treaties their ancestors signed with the British government in 1760 and 1761. The Supreme Court of Canada ruled in the 1999 Marshall decision that the treaties still form part of the law of Canada. Bob and William Payne were arrested on charges of obstruction in early May 2000 for attempting to reclaim Mi'kmaq lobster traps from an RCMP boat. Recently Bob has been serving with CPT in Columbia.

I continue my on-going work of retreats and training in the spirituality and practice of nonviolence. I try to stay awake to the demands of authentic long-term resistance to militarism and its brutal economy. Maintaining a rough balance between my writing and retreat work with my wage-earning trade work (drywalling) is at times a very difficult discipline. As I sometimes joke with my friends, "I've had to lay off my chauffeur, chef, housekeeper, secretary, and accountant."

Church walls
I recently met up with one of my nieces. We were able to engage in a much fuller conversation than is usually possible at the rare family gatherings where our paths barely cross. She is HIV positive. She is a joyful and spiritually centered young woman. At one point in our conversation she asserted, "I'm glad I had to face my mortality when I was young. It has helped me to mature spiritually." Though she did not grow up in the church, she is now in the process of becoming part of the Catholic Church. It was the freedom I sensed in her that made me see how authentic a faith decision this was for her.

Whether or not we're given the hard grace of facing our own physical mortality, coming to terms with death is how we come to that simple but profound insight: life is short. In that context, a relationship to the church must be lived in freedom; it cannot be left unexamined. It needs to remain a free choice. In conscience I only have two options in relation to war and the church. I can freely leave. Or I can enter so deeply into the life and mystery of the church that I yearn for it to be as free as I myself yearn to be. The false teaching of the Just War is a wall that dangerously confines and stunts that spiritual growth and freedom.

(Left to right) Anna Jarvis, Kay Barcley and Stephen Jarvis during a break at the trial

A short while ago John K. Stoner of *New Call to Peacemaking*, sent me information about a new initiative by the historic peace churches: "Every Church a Peace Church." If we took this vision seriously, how could we most effectively work towards such a transformation? I propose a process based on the model of the United Church of Canada's "Affirming Congregations."

If I walk by a United Church building that has the rainbow sign with the words "Affirming Congregation," I know that the members of that congregation took the time to go through a process of self-education and conversion in relationship to their lesbian sisters and gay brothers. At the end of that process, if there is a consensus, a congregation publicly declares that it fully welcomes anyone regardless of her or his sexual orientation. The rainbow sign becomes a public witness of both the renunciation of sexual discrimination and the nurturing of an inclusive faith community.

During the three-week public fast at Trinity-St. Paul's United Church (mentioned above), I became involved in a passionate conversation with members of the congregation. They saw an urgent need for their church to come to terms with its denial about its own particular role in perpetuating militarism and its brutal economy. They understood the importance of public renunciation of the Just War teaching; the importance of coming to terms with the public implications of love of enemy; and the importance of learning to use the powerful tools of the force of love we call nonviolence. "How could we change the bureaucracy of the whole United Church? It seems hopeless!" said one of them. That's when I thought of the United Church's "Affirming Congregation" process. It is a process that works from the ground up; one congregation at a time.

I think that in all the mainline churches it would be possible to apply such a process to the renunciation of war and the affirmation of gospel nonviolence. I propose that the symbol for the "Every Church a Peace Church" movement be the drawing commissioned for our Cross and Sword Witness: the striking image of the *Cross and Ploughshare* created by artist Christopher Reilly. Passing by this symbol on a church, one would know that it represented a congregation that had publicly renounced the false church teaching of Just War; a congregation affirming gospel nonviolence and apprenticing in the use of the powerful tools of resistance and conflict transformation; a congregation that was building nonviolent alternatives based on radical cooperation; a congregation in solidarity with global nonviolent movements such as the International Fellowship of Reconciliation; finally, a congregation exploring the mystery of love of enemy.

Freedom

Over the years, at least three different neighbours have seriously threatened me. One threatened my life for confronting serious abuse on our street. I've been disowned for refusing to disown a neighbour's enemy. Some have purposely broken my things. One slashed the tires of my bike and extinguished a lit cigarette on its seat. A number have lied to me. Some have stolen from me. Some have pounded on walls and ceilings in an attempt to intimidate a fellow neighbour. One young neighbour on heavy drugs threw garbage on my doorstep and yelled "I'll get you" because I had finally removed his motorcycle parts from my entrance (as he had promised to do over and over). These are all "ordinary Canadians."

In each case I have challenged myself to do all I could to live the mystery of love of enemy. Because of that I have grown spiritually. Many times my neighbour-enemy has been my teacher, revealing my own anger and fear. In all cases I have renounced the quest for victory and have worked for reconciliation, for some transformation of the conflict at hand. Because of that, I have become freer. In each case, there has indeed been a transformation of the conflict—sometimes to a dramatic degree. The young man who dumped garbage at my entrance and harassed me for days, unexpectedly came up to me and apologized—actually admitting "I've been on drugs for the last while," and showing me some child-like drawings he had just done.

Freedom has always been one of the greatest mysteries to me. We are free to love and we are free to hate. However difficult the choice may be, it remains a choice. The mystery of freedom encounters what at first seems merely a moral imperative: love your enemy. And yet, more fully understood, it is the *mystery of freedom* encountering the *mystery of love of enemy*. Mystery encountering mystery.

Mysteries are to be lived. We are not *as* One Body, we *are* One Body. When one part is hurt, all are hurt. We are that intimately connected—lover, friend or enemy. Yet we are free; free to destroy or nurture our interdependence. The most sanctioned rupture is the one between myself and my enemy. The most illusionary freedom is that which is based on the destruction of the enemy. The most radical freedom is the freedom found at the very heart of the mystery of love of enemy. And the enemy is everywhere—stranger, neighbour, co-worker, parent, spouse, child, lover or self. To be fully alive is to live the mystery of freedom at the very heart of the mystery of love of enemy; to do the emotional and spiritual work involved—individually and collectively; to enter more deeply into the depth and breadth of Love.

Slowly, I am unlearning the lie of my culture: love of enemy is no sexy; it does not sell; it is for naïve weaklings. Slowly I am unlearning the lie of the official church: love of enemy is just an ideal; an optional challenge to reach for the impossible in one's private life. At most, love of enemy is presented as a command only, not a life-giving mystery.

Slowly, I am learning that *not* to live the mystery of love of enemy is to be seriously stunted in spirit, in vision and in imagination. This mystery affects all we do—including our work of hospitality and resistance. To offer hospitality and to do resistance—even radical hospitality and radical resistance—from the wrong motives is spiritually unhealthy and dangerous. When hospitality or resistance is disconnected from love of enemy, what is it really about? When the crises and conflicts surface, will we have the spiritual resources needed?

"But you're just a drywaller!" What do you know about mysteries?" If these mysteries are not accessible to all of us, we are doomed.

"But you're a nice Canadian, not an ugly American. Isn't your resistance extreme?" Our lying myth of "Canada the peacemaker" keeps us in dangerous denial about the particular nature of Canadian militarism: cowardly acquiescence to the empire and hypocritical profiteering. War simply cannot be left to the self-proclaimed experts—military or political.

Every culture has a warrior tradition: Christian, Jewish, Muslim and Buddhist; Francophone Canadian, Anglophone Canadian and First Nations; Conservative Party, Liberal Party, New Democratic Party. Historically, we are all confronted with the same challenge: to perpetuate the Institution of War or begin a global apprenticeship in the other force. In a culture where the many do not confront the enemy within, the few are eventually sent to destroy the designated enemy without.

The more I pray for a deepening of compassion, the less willing I become to expend my energy *reacting* to the endless wars; the more I need to resist War itself. The more I try to stretch in faith, the more central a mystery love of enemy reveals itself to be.

A good Jesuit friend who had seriously considered joining our Cross and Sword witness expressed his hesitation by referring to the war memorial with the cross and sword as a "dead symbol." Others referred to it as "*just* a symbol."

A symbol is fully a symbol—not "just" a symbol. It may represent something significant or something quite insignificant. For me the Cross and Sword symbol was as significant as a statue depicting Christ napalming a child, raping an enemy, torturing a prisoner of war, or starving the already poor by throwing the people's money (taxes) down a sewer. They symbol of the Cross and Sword war memorial is that real for me. It is not just a symbol; it is *fully* a symbol of the blasphemy of war and of who we have become as mainline churches. It remains intact, well protected by state and church.

Confronting the Cross and Sword symbol was for me emotionally akin to the unearthing of mass graves. Both around the war memorial and over the mass graves, grass and flowers hide corruption. Not long ago a colour photo in the *Toronto Star* depicted a man and a woman trying to identify relatives among bound and mutilated corpses from a mass grave in Chechnya. The woman covers her mouth and nose with a cloth. The man has a full gas mask on. The terrible corruption beneath the quiet façade of grass and flowers has been exposed. Is the Cross and Sword a "dead symbol," or have we, as a culture, become spiritually numb?

Sometimes the wheels inside my brain and heart grind like bits of glass and blood at the sight of the relentless warmaking. After centuries of cheap prayers and expensive taxes, we have nearly perfected our killing machine: women and minorities are allowed into its ranks and offered a free career; a bottomless pit of taxpayers' money assures the ceaseless perfection of war's technology; and a perpetual war economy is so normalized that even the most progressive economists rarely make the connections between militarism and the globalization of poverty. Most mainstream economists build their impressive-sounding logic on sick premises, such as the expendability of the poor.

I never, ever chose this vocation of exposing and resisting War. It—Christ—kept confronting me. Resisting war has disrupted my life and those around me as surely as joining the warmaking would have. The hardest thing is that my personality does not lean towards "being against" or "resisting," but rather towards creating. I would rather spend my time doing works of mercy—without having to cry out; doing good work—without having to expose militarism; creating beauty—without facing my culture's sickness.

Recently I was relishing the energy of live music. Its raw power suddenly sliced through me, like a sharp knife, exposing vulnerable emotions: "What have I been doing all these years resisting War—instead of creating music, growing gardens?" So many "failures." So few "successes." So little personal "security".

And yet, I experience an indestructible joy, beyond any temporary happiness. I experience fruitfulness, beyond all success or failure. The War Child left at the doorway of my soul long ago, has taken me into the life-giving mystery of love of enemy. I will never be the same. She has the most urgent message of all to give to my culture about poverty and freedom. I have learned that the same One who is with the War Child in her unjust suffering and death will be with me in my own suffering and death. Put simply, freedom has taken root in me.

I have learned that no prison can take that freedom away. Nor the threat of death. I can think of no greater honour than to die resisting war. Yet it is not all what I most desire. What **do** I desire? My desire is freedom—far beyond the bloodied walls of fear and hatred of enemy erected by prison or church; far beyond myself and my small community of friends. My desire is for the freedom of the whole of the Beloved Community. Directly connected to this desire for freedom is my love for the church community.

My love for the church is—like my love of God—either an irrelevant sentiment or a vital part of being fully human: living a relationship with God in community with sisters and brothers for the love of all humanity and all creation. I dearly love my widest community: friends who know nothing of the church's inner riches; friends who can only feel the hurt that the church represents; friends of other faiths. But I have a burning love for the sheer mystery of church as faith community. My soul needs the nourishment found in this mystical, indestructible home. It is where I live my greatest freedom.

Saltiness returning?
We have begun to change as a church community. Salt regaining its saltiness? Signs of conversion are all around us: the *International Fellowship of Reconciliation (IFOR)*, originally a Christian movement, now the world's oldest interfaith network of groups and individuals committed to active nonviolence, continues to grow with branches in over 40 countries, on every continent, and with the active participation of many church groups; *Servicio Paz Y Justicia (SERPAJ)*, affiliated with the IFOR, is the organized network of active nonviolence in Central and Latin America; the *Fellowship of Reconciliation in the United States (FOR-USA)*, whose roots are also Christian, now encompasses the *Muslim Peace Fellowship* and the *Jewish Peace Fellowship*; the *Canadian Religious Conference* publicly commits itself to gospel nonviolence as the force with which to do justice; individual religious communities are beginning to name nonviolence as a constitutive element of their communal vision; *Pace e Bene*, a Franciscan centre for nonviolence, is thriving; bishops like Tom Gumbleton pay the price for refusing to cooperate with the state's militarism and for renouncing the Catholic Church's false teaching of

Just War; *Pax Christi International* nurtures active nonviolence within the Catholic Church; the *Anglican Pacifist Fellowship* in England is a voice advocating the return to pacifist orthodoxy in the church; in Montreal, the *Centre de ressources sur la non-violence* is partly supported by Franciscans; *Christian Peacemaker Teams (CPT—including CPT-Canada)* risk the "yes" of accompaniment and the "no" of intervention in areas of conflict at home and abroad; small faith communities persist in nonviolent resistance along with the works of mercy. And there is more—much, much more.

Imagine expensive, bloodied Sword turning into Ploughshare for the sick, starving, uneducated and unemployed. Imagine the Sword at the heart of the church turning into Ploughshare. Imagine conversion: from renunciation to liberation. Imagine the enemy revealing our truer self as a church community. Imagine the enemy revealing the depth and breadth of Christ's justice, mercy and reconciliation—Christ's freedom. Imagine the enemy revealing the fuller face of Love.

www.ingramcontent.com/pod-product-compliance
Lightning Source LLC
LaVergne TN
LVHW021715060526
838200LV00050B/2675